D0997343

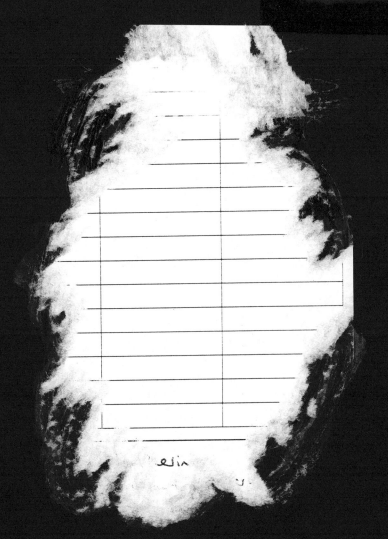

The
ORNAMENTAL
HERB GARDEN

The
ORNAMENTAL
HERB GARDEN

From windowboxes to knot gardens

Catherine Mason

conran
OCTOPUS

First published in 1997 by
Conran Octopus Limited
37 Shelton Street
London WC2H 9HN

Text copyright © Catherine Mason 1997
Design and layout copyright © Conran Octopus
1997

Commissioning Editor: Stuart Cooper
Project Editor: Helen Woodhall
Copy Editor: Annie Lee
Designer: Peter Butler
Illustrators: Lesley Craig, Liz Pepperell
Picture Research: Helen Fickling
Production: Mano Mylvaganam
Index: Helen Snaith

ISBN 1 85029 912 9

British Library Cataloguing-in-Publication Data
A catalogue record for this book is available from
the British Library

Printed in Hong Kong by
Wing King Tong Co. Ltd.

PAGE 1: Rosa gallica *var.* officinalis *and* Borago
officinalis.
PAGE 2: *Dense planting in an English country
herb garden.*
PAGE 3: *Clipped herbs echo the rounded shape of
weathered stone.*
PAGE 4: *Exuberant marigolds emphasize the
formality of the box topiary.*

CONTENTS

THE APPEAL OF HERB GARDENS

Herb gardening combines all aspects of plant-growing, from the practical and utilitarian to the aesthetic. A herb garden can be the most beautiful of places, and the natural limitations it imposes bring a unity and coherence to the overall picture that are sometimes lacking in gardens which try to incorporate a bit of everything. It will provide both flavouring and visual enhancement for food, a supply of fresh and unusual garnishing material for several months of the year, even simple remedies for common ailments, if so desired.

Herb plants do not generally have large bright flowers, although there are of course exceptions, and the quieter tones can make for a tranquil contemplative garden, with the emphasis on the more subtle and less transient delights of texture, foliage and perfume. A garden should stimulate and soothe all the senses, not just the eyes, and many herbs are wonderfully aromatic. On a hot summer's day a well-stocked herb garden alive with the buzz of pollinating insects, the scent of lavender and the song of birds is a lovely place to be.

My intention in writing this book has been to approach herbs from the garden-maker's point of view. A great deal has been written about herbal remedies, beauty treatments and the culinary uses of herbs; less about their value as garden plants and how to grow them. I wanted to gather together all the information a gardener would need to plan, design, plant and maintain an ornamental herb garden, avoiding at least some of the pitfalls, and making a garden which would be both beautiful and useful. I have adopted a rather loose definition of the term 'herb', which I take to mean any plant which is now, or has ever been, grown for its medicinal or flavouring properties. I have also concentrated on those herbs which I consider to be garden-worthy plants in their own right, irrespective of any other qualities they might possess.

Mediterranean herbs such as santolina, lavender, sage and oregano all flourish in the gravel of the sheltered herb garden at Hintlesham Hall, Suffolk, England.

DESIGN AND DECORATION

THERE ARE MANY FACTORS TO TAKE INTO ACCOUNT WHEN EMBARKING ON THE PROCESS OF PLANNING, DESIGNING AND DECORATING A HERB GARDEN. THE KEY TO CREATING A HERB GARDEN THAT SUITS YOU AND YOUR NEEDS IS TO TAKE THE PROCESS STEP BY STEP, AT ALL STAGES ASSESSING AND RE-ASSESSING THE EFFECT YOU WANT TO ACHIEVE. THE SPACE YOU HAVE AVAILABLE, THE PHYSICAL CHARACTERISTICS OF THAT SPACE, AND THE TIME AND RESOURCES YOU HAVE AT YOUR DISPOSAL WILL ALL HAVE A BEARING ON THE GARDEN THAT YOU CREATE.

*A peaceful herb garden sheltered by tall hedges, with clipped
box parterres and a stylish metal seat, provides a formal contrast to
the wilder landscape beyond.*

Planning a Herb Garden

Designing a herb garden from scratch can seem a daunting prospect, but when the process is broken down into its constituent parts it becomes more manageable. This chapter examines each of the essential tasks in the order in which they are best carried out.

SURVEYING THE SITE

Before thinking about the type of garden you want to make, it is sensible to establish precisely what is already in place, any items which must remain unaltered, and also any which would be better changed or removed. While it may be tempting to start immediately on the site assessment or design phases, especially if you have lived with the existing garden for several years, it is actually a very useful exercise to set aside any preconceptions and make a true and accurate record of what is there, rather than what you think is there.

Measuring and plotting a level rectangular site presents few problems, but where the shape is irregular, some simple surveying techniques are needed. Divide the garden into smaller sections using obvious fixed points such as trees, paths or walls, and measure each section individually, before amalgamating them on the plan. Make plenty of rough sketches as you work, jotting measurements on them as you progress.

Where the shape is very irregular, a technique known as triangulation is used. It is normally possible to use a house wall or straight garden fence as the base line from which to measure out fixed triangular shapes which can be used to plot irregular outlines. If not, use a tape-measure laid out and fixed along the ground as a base line, and measure from that. To plot a curved boundary, another option is to take a series of parallel offset measurements out to the boundary at right angles from the base line, at measured intervals.

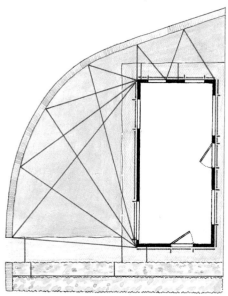

To create a scale plan, measure triangles from the house out to the boundary at intervals. Plot to scale on paper, and join the boundary points freehand, for a reasonably accurate scale drawing of curves.

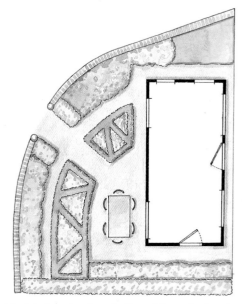

The finished design, showing the line of the path altered to draw attention to the view from the window. Herb parterres, beds and the seating area are fitted in around this.

DRAWING PLANS

Before doing any work in the garden use the survey measurements to make a scale plan of the site. For an average-sized garden a scale of 1 in 50 is usually about right. On the plan, mark the position of the house, and of all doors and windows. It is also helpful to plot existing trees, including their canopy size, drains, manhole covers, paths, paving, walls, fences and any changes in level. Indicate any garden features you wish to keep. A direction indicator – usually an arrow pointing north, is vital, since aspect has a major influence over light levels, which determine what can be planted. This plan is used as the basis for the garden design, and we will return to it later, during the design phase.

The sundial draws the eye inwards, away from the perimeter, and provides a satisfying contrast to the soft outlines of the plants.

SITE ASSESSMENT

Whether located in the country or in a city, a garden forms part of a wider landscape. The view from it may be a garden's greatest asset, but if the immediate vicinity is unattractive you will probably wish to screen off as much as possible, creating a garden with an inward focus. For most of us the reality falls somewhere in between, but it is certainly worth standing in the middle of your site and taking a good look round to see if there might be an external feature visible that is worth emphasizing. Take your time, be systematic and look out of the garden in all directions. You may also spot something previously unnoticed that you would prefer to have concealed. Look out on your proposed garden from all the house windows which overlook it, and try to see everything that is there. Most of us see very selectively, mentally editing out things we prefer not to look at. Photographs are an enormous help in this regard, as they invariably highlight any eyesores.

It is also worth making a tour of the locality to assess how visible the garden will be within its surroundings. Temporary markers, such as canes with bright plastic bags attached, can be inserted at key positions in the garden site to assist the process. Country gardens, in particular, can strike a jarring note if they are insensitively designed.

It is important to consider carefully the physical characteristics of your herb garden site, by which I mean such things as shelter from wind, aspect (the direction it faces), the amount of sun and shade it receives, the soil type, rainfall and temperature range.

Most of the aromatic herbs need an open, sunny site, with relatively free-draining soil, whereas many salad herbs enjoy more lush conditions and will tolerate some shade. It is a disheartening waste of time and effort to attempt to grow plants which do not suit the conditions you are able to provide. Much better to plant only those species you can grow well, and enjoy watching them flourish.

In the northern hemisphere, south-facing gardens are generally sunny and north-facing gardens shady, and in the southern hemisphere vice versa, but there is no substitute for observing your site at different times of year. If you have snowfall, note where it melts first and last, as these are the warmest and coldest parts of the garden, respectively. There may be some areas which receive no sun at all for several months of the year. Shade patterns differ markedly between winter and summer, as the winter sun is lower in the sky. Local factors such as large trees or buildings can create shade at ground level whatever the aspect of the garden. Buildings, walls and fences can also create rain shadows, and the soil in their immediate vicinity may be very dry as a result.

Protection from wind is vital, especially if you plan to grow some of the taller herbs. Before you do any planting, observe the direction of the prevailing wind and decide how you are going to provide the necessary shelter. If shelter will be coming from a newly planted hedge you may need to erect some temporary windbreak netting, for the benefit both of the hedging plants and of your herbs. It may look awful for a while, but is likely to mean the difference between life and death for your plants.

There are four main soil types: sand, clay, silt and loam. Heavy, sticky clay and light, free-draining sand are easy to recognize. Loam is beautiful: dark and crumbly, yet moisture retentive, and if you have it you are fortunate. Silt is the most

ABOVE: *Raised herb beds are supported by low wattle fencing.*
Although less permanent than brick, they will last for a few years.
OPPOSITE: *Deep shadows accentuate the lines of this herbal knot,*
adding a touch of drama to a formal garden.

difficult to identify. Compress a ball of soil in your hand and
rub it between your fingers. The texture of silt is slightly soapy
with a hint of grittiness, not quite so sticky as clay, but like
clay it is easily compacted if you walk on it in wet weather.

Most herbs are quite adaptable, but few will tolerate being
waterlogged. If standing water is a problem, you will need to
do something to improve drainage. This can range from
incorporating coarse grit into a clay or silt soil, to full-scale

digging of land drains, depending on the severity of the problem. Observe your site throughout the autumn and winter
months before deciding what, if any, drainage measures are
necessary. It is all too easy to be lulled into a false sense of
security by a dry summer.

Before any planting is carried out, it is also wise to test the
soil pH, using a proprietary kit or meter. Soil may be acid,
alkaline or neutral, and most herbs will flourish in soil that is
somewhere between neutral and slightly acid (pH 7.0 and
6.0). Measurements should be taken in various parts of the
garden, as acidity can vary quite considerably even over a short
distance. Generally it is easier to reduce the acidity of soil, by
the addition of lime, than to increase it, although the latter
can be achieved over a period of years by adding plenty of
acidic organic material such as leafmould. If you have not
already done so, dig a hole at this stage to establish the depth
of the topsoil and check on soil structure and drainage.

Even where the space for herbs is strictly limited, much
can be achieved. In my current garden, twenty-five different
herbs are grown in a small raised bed less than 1.5m (5ft)
square, which is sufficient for all our culinary needs. A raised
bed gives the plants the good drainage most of them need
and, when it is small enough to cultivate from the sides, can
be very densely planted, both suppressing weeds and enabling
heavier cropping than is possible with traditional rows.

The boundary between herbs and ornamental plants is
quite blurred, and incorporating herbs into more general
ornamental planting presents few problems. Choose herbs to
fit the prevailing conditions, and exclude the more invasive
genera. Most herbs can be harvested by cutting a few leaves at
a time, so sudden gaps in the planting need not occur.

The rich soil conditions typical of vegetable gardens are
suited only to the more leafy salad herbs. Parsley, sorrel, chives
and rocket will thrive, but herbs from warmer climates generally need a more spartan diet. Again, the importance of
matching the plant to its growing conditions cannot be over-
emphasized. Herbs such as curled parsley and chives make
good decorative edging plants in the vegetable garden.

HOW THE GARDEN WILL BE USED

Consider how the garden will be used before making major decisions. It is common sense to grow herbs for cooking close to the kitchen, but will there be convenient access to all areas of culinary planting via hard surfaces? At what time of day will the garden mainly be used? You may want to position a bench facing the sunset, with night-scented herbs in the vicinity. Pale-coloured leaves and flowers show up better at night than dark ones. If the garden will be much used after dark it may even be worth installing lighting. Where necessary a water feature can be effective in masking traffic noise.

Will the safety of children or animals be a consideration? If so, poisonous or stinging plants should be excluded, or at least grown well away from paths; boundaries may need to be

secure, and any water features must be very carefully chosen. A more general safety consideration concerns slippery surfaces. Use wooden decking or timber-stepping stones with caution in regions with a damp climate. You can buy decking with grooves cut into the wood, which alleviates slipperiness to some extent, but log-section stepping-stones can be lethal in wet weather. Chicken wire stapled to smooth wooden surfaces may help, but it does little for the aesthetic effect.

Try to be realistic about how much time will be available for maintenance after the initial planting. Clipping hedges, weeding, sowing seeds, thinning seedlings and watering containers can take up a considerable amount of time. If bricks or paving slabs are not set in cement, they will require regular weeding or spraying, yet an unbroken expanse of path can appear very harsh. A compromise might be to leave planting pockets at intervals, for a softening effect.

Where time is severely restricted it is possible to plant only perennial herbs which come up year after year, and those annuals which obligingly sow themselves, thus saving you the trouble, but even with this approach some maintenance will be necessary. Shrubby perennials such as sages and lavenders need annual pruning, self-sown seedlings may have to be moved, and regular weeding will need to be carried out.

Opposite above: This elegant dining terrace is conveniently close to the house, and forms a transitional area, linking the house and herb garden into a seamless whole. The furniture is graceful but unobtrusive, and the weathered timber of the table top complements the house timbers perfectly. The shape of the herb beds echoes the grid pattern of the timber framing, reinforcing the link between house and garden.
Opposite below: These herb beds are small enough to be accessible from the surrounding hard paths, so even in wet weather the cook can gather herbs without getting muddy feet.
Top: This apple pergola and lavender-edged path lead the eye irresistibly to the rustic gate, and frame the view of the lake beyond.
Above: Dark paving slabs with gravel – a stylish mix of hard landscaping materials.

DESIGN CONSIDERATIONS
The age and style of the house should be considered when deciding on a garden design. Do you want to plant a garden in keeping with an old house, perhaps containing only plants that were cultivated at the time the house was built? Most formal layouts for herb gardens are adaptations of ancient designs which might be inappropriate for a modern house. In a more contemporary setting, it might be better to choose a less retrospective theme, perhaps even something inspired by modern art, such as the Mondrian grid (see page 16), on which to base the design.

Structure and scale are the most important elements in garden design. Get them wrong at the outset and no amount of planting will cover your mistakes. If you take the time to

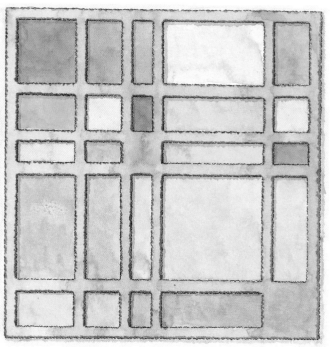

This design for a small herb garden, enclosed by a protective hedge, is a variation on an age-old theme. The sundial, a traditional herb garden centrepiece, makes for a contemplative, inward-looking atmosphere, which is accentuated by the intimate seating.

Many formal designs for herb gardens are retrospective, and not suited to a modern house. Inspired by the work of Dutch modernist painter Piet Mondrian, this asymmetrical knot of low hedges and herbs interspersed with gravel strikes a more contemporary note.

get the bare bones of the garden – the proportions, the vistas, and so on – right, the rest is comparatively easy, or at least more amenable to alteration!

The garden should, of course, be in scale with the house. The elements within the garden also need to be in scale with the garden as a whole. For instance: if there is space only for a narrow gravel path, use fine rather than coarse gravel.

Gardens are for people, and should be scaled accordingly. Paths, steps, seats, and so on should be of a size which can be used with comfort. If these elements are too large, visitors may feel dwarfed and ill-at-ease, if too small, they will feel uncomfortably cramped.

Whether designing a garden from scratch or merely making alterations, it is often helpful to think in terms of creating garden pictures. In a picture, everything is carefully selected

and arranged, there is nothing superfluous or unintentional. So it should be in a garden. Try to banish distractions that diminish the overall desired effect. Gardens need focal points such as ornamental features or furniture. They lend a sense of completion, rounding off the picture. Only one focal point should predominate at any one time, otherwise conflicting demands on the attention will feel unsettling. Focal points may be used to direct the attention, drawing the visitor further into the garden to explore, or leading the eye out of the garden towards a more distant 'borrowed view'.

In formal herb gardens attention is often focused inwards to a central feature such as a pool, sundial or urn. Try to ensure that such features are in scale with the rest of the garden. It is easy to choose something too small, which simply looks lost when placed in its intended setting.

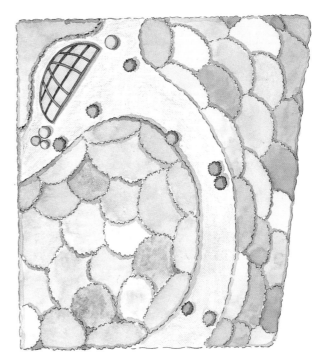

A low knot of aromatic herbs, designed to be viewed from above, perhaps from a terrace within the garden, or a balcony or upstairs window. The knot outlines of santolina need to be kept tightly clipped, as a contrast to the more sprawling herbs also grown.

In this informal herb garden, the edge between the gravel path and herb borders is left deliberately blurred, with herbs encouraged to seed into the gravel. The rustic arbour is sited to catch the evening sun – a place to sit and relax at the end of the day.

A beautiful ornament or feature can often benefit from 'framing'. At its simplest, a pair of matching pots either side of an entrance can be very effective. More elaborate methods might include arches or doorways, which could be fashioned from topiary or hard materials. Trees may be pleached, their branches trained and clipped into aerial hedges, their trunks framing a view of the distant landscape; the uprights of a pergola can be used in a similar manner. The effect is to lead the eye, to focus attention on what is visible within the frame. Repetition reinforces this attention-focusing effect. Plants, containers, statuary, garden architecture – any of these elements will, if repeated, have a similar effect: the recurrence of a key plant at intervals along the sides of a path draws the eye along it to the end. Whatever is used needs to stand out in some way from the garden background.

The important elements of surprise and drama can be introduced in various ways, perhaps by enclosing the herb garden so that it cannot be seen from outside. Mediterranean gardens make great use of the interplay of light and shade, and even in countries where the light is less intense, we could exploit it more. Shadows cast by trellis or pergolas add drama to a garden scene that is no less valuable for being fleeting.

When designing paths, try to make them lead somewhere rather than petering out into a dead end. Think about which areas will receive the heaviest foot traffic and plan accordingly. If paths do not follow the shortest route between two points people will take short cuts unless you prevent them by putting a large enough obstacle in the way. Think whether you will need to get a wheelbarrow, or other wide equipment along paths, before deciding on their dimensions.

HERB GARDEN STYLES

The majority of ornamental herb gardens are formal in style. There is good reason for this, in that herbs are a disparate group of plants, some of which have sprawling habits. A collection can easily look bitty and incoherent unless subjected to the discipline of a formal layout. A well-planned evergreen framework can be used to reinforce the symmetry of any formal layout, and retains interest throughout the winter months when many herbs are dormant.

For a formal plant parterre or knot garden use one or more of the low-growing evergreen shrubby herbs, such as box, to delineate the outline.

Informal herb gardens, loosely planted with no obvious structure, are more difficult to design successfully. For this type of garden to look attractive, some sort of evergreen 'backbone' planting is usually incorporated and a high level of maintenance is required. One option is to use the herbaceous border or island bed arrangement, planted solely with herbs.

DESIGNING ON PAPER

Return now to the base plan made at the time of surveying and make several photocopies of it before drawing in the new design. Alternatively, overlay the base plan with tracing paper to try out new design elements. Use paper tape to stick the plans to a drawing board. For the sake of clarity, do not try to cram too much detail on to the master plan. Use it to work out a pleasing overall structure for the herb garden, and to mark key design features such as hedges, knots, paths, seats, sundials, and so on. In all but the smallest gardens draw separate detailed planting plans for each herb bed.

FROM THEORY INTO PRACTICE

Time spent on site, thinking about and trying to visualize the garden is never wasted. Move around the plot with a copy of the plan, and go over each part of the design methodically, trying to imagine the mature effect. Use canes or other props to help in visualizing heights and positions of key plants or features. Think about what will be obscured from view or

OPPOSITE ABOVE: *Golden oregano spills out over the edge of the gravel path in this relaxed planting, and leads the eye gently towards the cool inviting shade of the tree seat, which forms an effective focal point.*

OPPOSITE BELOW: *This very naturalistic scree garden looks as if it has been there forever, but in fact it provides an object lesson in matching the needs of plants to their environment. The thymes, thrift and other sun-loving herbs are obviously thriving in conditions of near-perfect drainage.*

BELOW RIGHT: *A study in green – sculptural box topiary with a well-placed self-sown foxglove. Dramatic shadows emphasize the formal lines of the topiary.*

revealed by the mature garden. Do this from different parts of the site, and from the house too, when appropriate, and do it at the times of day when the garden is most likely to be used.

If there are to be new walls, fences or hedges, use canes to check the sight lines, making sure that those things you wish to conceal will really be hidden. This is particularly necessary if you are designing a concealed entrance in a hedge or trellis – get it wrong and the effect is totally lost. Remember to check the sight lines from seating areas.

Above all do not rush this process. Only when you feel satisfied with all aspects of your design on paper should you begin the work on site.

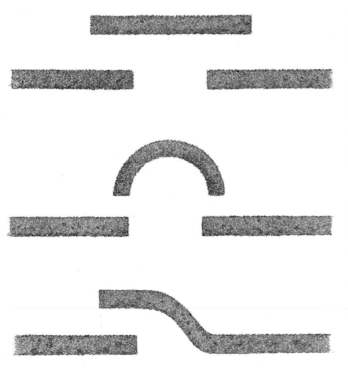

ABOVE: *There are many variations on the theme of concealed entrances, both in terms of the material employed and the plan used. Hedges, walls or trellis can all be used in various patterns, but first mock up your plans on site and make sure that any objects you wish to conceal will not be visible.*

Hard Landscaping

Hard landscaping forms the basic, unchanging garden framework of paths, walls and other structures. It is both expensive and long-lasting, so should be designed and constructed with great care, as mistakes can be costly to rectify. It is only practical to do the hard landscaping before the planting is carried out, to avoid damage to plants.

DESIGN CONSIDERATIONS

It is important to select materials that harmonize both with the house and with the wider surroundings. If in doubt, look first at local materials when planning hard landscaping projects. Most regions have quite specific building traditions, and it often seems that local materials have an aura of rightness in a particular environment. In designated conservation areas there may be regulations governing the types of hard landscaping material permitted. In many countries, planners have become increasingly strict about perpetuating vernacular building styles in recent years. Before going to any great expense, it is vital to check the local regulations.

Using the same materials throughout different areas of the garden gives a sense of order, continuity and smoothness of transition that is much harder to achieve with a piecemeal approach. If there are to be gravel paths in different areas of the garden, make sure the same gravel is used throughout. It may sound trivial, but this sort of attention to detail can make a huge difference to the end result. Mixing different materials calls for restraint. A path made of stone slabs set in gravel can look marvellous, but add bricks and rope tiles too, and the end result is a visual muddle.

The hard elements in a garden should never be permitted to dominate the plants. Large expanses of hard material such as paving can be softened by allowing billowing plants to spill over the edges, by leaving planting pockets within the paving area, or by massing plants in containers. Walls, fences and trellis should be clothed with climbing plants or wall shrubs.

Hard landscaping materials can be broadly divided into two categories, natural and synthetic. The level of maintenance they require is a major consideration, and varies from almost none to a great deal. Make sure you know what you are letting yourself in for. Natural materials, such as stone, generally weather better than synthetics, but concrete and reconstituted stone vary considerably in this regard. Do some research and try to see a weathered example of material you are considering that has been installed for a few years.

Stone has a timeless quality which rarely looks out of place in the garden. It is expensive but durable, requiring little maintenance after the initial building or installation.

ABOVE: *Creeping thymes soften the edges of these informal stone steps, and release their perfume when crushed underfoot.*
OPPOSITE: *Richly textured paths, made from a mixture of old bricks and stone, are a lovely foil for the relaxed herb planting.*

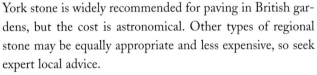

York stone is widely recommended for paving in British gardens, but the cost is astronomical. Other types of regional stone may be equally appropriate and less expensive, so seek expert local advice.

Although bricks can be used for building and for paving, not all are suitable for both purposes. Bricks for paving need to be especially durable to resist the wear and tear of foot traffic and the elements. As with stone, the initial outlay is high, but subsequent maintenance costs relatively low.

Cobbles are smooth, water-worn stones, often set in concrete and used to add interest to paved areas. They can look wonderful, but are uncomfortable and sometimes slippery to

ABOVE LEFT: *A bark chip path and rustic wattle fence are perfect complements to this lush planting.*
BELOW LEFT: *This scene of studied formality relies on perfect clipping of the symmetrically placed topiary domes.*
ABOVE: *The golden hop,* Humulus lupulus *'Aureus', looks striking against the dark blue of the low picket fence.*

walk on, so are best confined to small areas. They need to be laid carefully to minimize their inherent unevenness, and the process is laborious. Make sure they are set closely together – too far apart and the effect is ruined. Cobbles of contrasting colours can be laid in patterns to give a mosaic effect.

Gravel is one of the easiest of hard landscaping materials for an inexperienced person to work with. Gravel paths are often used in herb gardens to give a relaxed feel to the design, but they do need regular maintenance. Many plants seed readily into gravel, and regular weeding will be necessary.

Wood is incredibly versatile, and can be used in an almost infinite number of ways in the garden, from the casual informality of bark chip paths to the most elaborate formal trellis. Wooden structures, fences and trellis need periodic applications of preservative, so while the initial cost may seem low compared to other materials, maintenance can be expensive and time-consuming. Wood that is in direct contact with soil will rot in a few years, irrespective of how thoroughly it has been treated with preservative, so wooden posts are best set in concrete or coarse gravel.

Concrete paving and building materials are available preformed in a huge range of shapes and colours, many of which are very unattractive. The worst effects come from its overuse. The addition of an aggregate such as coarse gravel or small stones to the mix results in a more interesting, less obviously synthetic surface.

The range of reclaimed and recycled materials suitable for hard landscaping is on the increase. Disused railway sleepers have long been a stand-by of cost-conscious garden designers, and are still available. Architectural salvage companies and demolition firms are fertile hunting grounds for old bricks and building stone, mellowed with the patina of age. Bargains may be found, but it is more likely that the price will approach, or even exceed, that of the new equivalent. Given that old materials will probably look nicer than new, and be of similar or better quality, this is not unreasonable.

CONSTRUCTION BASICS

Where complicated hard landscaping work is called for, perhaps involving changes of level, it is best to use a contractor unless you are confident that you have the skills to cope. Less extensive work, however, as outlined here, is not beyond the capabilities of a reasonably fit, practical and intelligent adult.

Land drains Herbs will not thrive in waterlogged soil. If drainage problems cannot be alleviated by soil cultivation, constructing raised beds or simply mounding up the soil, more radical measures are called for. Rubble drains are probably adequate for draining the relatively small area occupied by most herb gardens. Dig trenches 60–90cm (2–3ft) deep and 30cm (1ft) wide, with a minimum fall of 1 in 200, leading to a watercourse or soakaway. These are conventionally arranged in a herringbone system, but on an average-sized site this would not be necessary. A single trench across the site, leading into a soakaway would be adequate. For a larger area, the spacing between the trenches depends on soil type: 4.5m (15ft) apart for clay, 7.5m (25ft) for loam and 12m (40ft) for sandy soils is a good rule of thumb. Where the herringbone system is employed, the side drains should meet the main drains at an angle of about 60 degrees. Half fill the

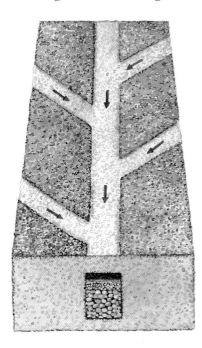

Waterlogged soil is anathema to herbs. In a simple herringbone land drain system, rubble drains should slope gently downhill into a water course or soakaway.

trenches with rubble and top this with a layer of coarse gravel, then with inverted turves or water-permeable ground-cover plastic, before replacing topsoil.

Soakaway To make a soakaway, dig a hole up to 1.8m (6ft) deep and wide. Line the sides with unmortared bricks or stones, and fill with rubble to within 30cm (1ft) of the soil surface. As with the drains, top with a layer of coarse gravel followed by inverted turves or water-permeable ground-cover plastic, then replace the topsoil.

Irrigation systems The design and installation of a sophisticated irrigation system is probably best left to a specialist contractor, but a system of porous pipes, either laid on the surface or buried in the soil before planting is begun, is a relatively low-tech, efficient alternative. The water is delivered directly to the roots where it is needed, so very little is lost by surface evaporation, and leaf splashing, which may cause scorching, is avoided. When buried, the pipes are completely unobtrusive and are invaluable for establishing long-term planting such as hedges and shrubs, but bear in mind their susceptibility to accidental damage from digging.

Place the pipes about 75cm (2½ft) apart, either on the soil surface or buried about 15cm (6in) deep. Either method will provide complete coverage. The runs should be no more than 50m (55yd), or 100m (110yd) if there is a water supply from both ends. They can be connected to orthodox hosepipes with standard fittings.

Paths and paved areas Solid paths and patios, made from brick, stone or concrete pavers, need solid foundations. Where there will be only light pedestrian traffic, paving may be laid on an 8cm (3in) bed of firmed sand. In areas of heavier traffic, where wheelbarrows or garden machinery will be in use, foundations should consist of a layer of consolidated hardcore, followed by sand or dry mix mortar. There should be a slight fall of about 1 in 40 from one side of the paving to the other, directing water into an adjoining planting area or a gully. Gravel paths should be laid over a layer of compacted hardcore (for which you will need to hire a compactor), and need to be edged. Brick, stone, log-rolls or rope

Stone or concrete paving slabs should be laid on a layer of sand or cement over compacted hardcore.

A gravel path is contained by treated wooden retaining boards held in place by pegs at 1m (3ft) intervals.

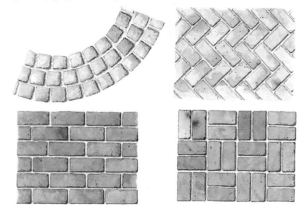

Bricks or granite sets can be arranged in various ways. Herringbone patterns suggest movement and look particularly good in paths.

tiles could be set in concrete foundations, or a strong, preservative-treated retaining board held in place by wooden pegs.

Raised beds Raised beds do not have to be very high to reap the benefits of improved drainage – even 15cm (6in) will make a difference. They can be constructed from brick, stone, treated wooden boards supported with pegs, log rolls, rustic timber posts inserted vertically into the earth, and so on. If brick or stone is used, a poured concrete foundation should be laid. Bricks must be mortared into place, but with stone there is a choice. If left unmortared, stone walling should have a slight inward batter (slope) for greater stability.

Fences and trellis Permeable fences are generally better than solid ones. A solid barrier takes the full force of the wind, and is thus more prone to damage. It may also create air turbulence in the very area it was intended to protect. A permeable barrier slows the wind speed without either of these drawbacks. Growing climbers or wall shrubs against the fence will

ABOVE: *This simple raised bed is made from treated timber, supported by wooden pegs hammered into the ground.*
BELOW LEFT: *A fence of living willow gives protection from wind.*

alleviate any loss of privacy. Hurdles made from hazel or willow filter the wind and form a visually solid screen, but might look incongruous in an urban setting. Country gardeners may be able to gather coppice wood, which can make attractive, low-cost fencing when nailed to a supporting framework.

The principles of fence erection are similar, whatever material is used. Posts, usually wooden, are sunk into the ground at intervals dictated either by the dimensions of the fence panels or by the type of framework under construction. The higher the fence, and the more solid it is, the deeper the posts should be buried. A 1.8m (6ft) fence should be supported by posts buried to a depth of 60–90cm (2–3ft). Fence posts may be driven directly into the ground, but are best bedded in concrete, or in proprietary hollow metal supports which are set in concrete. This prolongs their life and facilitates maintenance: it is much easier to replace a single fence section than the posts supporting it. The panels or framework are then attached either with proprietary fixings, nails, or, in the case of hurdles, strong wire.

Unpainted wooden fencing or trellis needs to be treated every two to three years with a preservative which is not toxic to plants, although as the range of colours available is quite restricted, exterior-grade paint may be a more suitable choice.

Furniture and Decoration

Herb gardens often incorporate some form of ornamentation or furniture, usually of a fairly modest nature, unless the garden is especially large. Something obviously man-made, like an urn or a statue, acts as a focus of attention, drawing the eye and making a garden scene appear composed and orderly, rather than a mere jumble of plants. Garden furniture serves a practical purpose, but its hard lines also act as a foil for the softness of the herb plantings.

STYLE CONSIDERATIONS

Most herb gardens are relatively small, making it especially important to maintain coherence of style. Pay attention to details: for instance, ensure that all your pots are of the same material, such as terracotta. Think about whether the decorative elements complement one another – do not put a very sleek, modern-looking seat under a rustic arbour, or at least do not do so by accident.

Where the herb garden immediately adjoins the house, try to make the transition from indoors to outdoors as smooth as possible by creating a visual link between the two. This might merely be a matter of using the same shade of paint for house door and garden seat, or it could be something quite ambitious, such as the echoing of a gable shape in topiary.

A well-chosen focal point brings a sense of completion to the garden picture: furniture or garden ornamentation often fulfils this role. A focal point is something which stands out from its immediate surroundings and so catches the eye. Bear in mind that the attention of the observer should not be divided by competing focal points visible from any one spot. If multiple decorative elements will be visible, make sure they complement rather than compete with each other, leading the eye smoothly onwards.

Objects such as urns, pots, finials, topiary and obelisks are often used in pairs to frame a garden picture or a good view, or to emphasize a gateway. A single imposing ornament, such

TOP: *This wooden bird, carved by D.J. Smith, is one of a pair of charming trellis finials at Brook Cottages in Hampshire, England.*
ABOVE: *These gates make highly original use of tree and shrub prunings. They manage both to blend into and to stand out from the garden picture with great subtlety and wit.*
OPPOSITE: *Wattle is an attractive and cost-effective construction material for a country garden.*

LEFT: *If painted a paler colour, this elegant summerhouse might seem too dominant in a garden setting.*
OPPOSITE ABOVE: *Attractively weathered old bell jars add to the romance of this timeless garden scene.*
OPPOSITE BELOW: *An inviting seat concludes the view along the lavender-lined path.*

CONTAINERS

When buying containers for planting, choose large ones, since small pots may need watering more than once a day in hot weather and are generally much harder work to maintain. If you opt for terracotta, buy frostproof pots if they are to remain outdoors in a frost-prone region. Lead is fiendishly expensive and not terribly portable, but it looks marvellous, complementing foliage colours like nothing else. Stone is even more expensive than lead, but again looks terrific.

If the budget will not run to new pots or containers, there are plenty of other options: old metal or plastic buckets (with holes for drainage), colanders, baby baths, old sinks, large tins, florist's buckets and numerous other objects can all be recycled as plant pots and given a coat of exterior-grade paint in a sympathetic shade, to unify what might otherwise be a rather random collection.

SEATING

Herb gardens are wonderful places in which to relax, and it is worth giving careful thought to the position of seating. Would you appreciate a place to sit and watch the sunset, drink in hand, after a hard day's work? A shaded outdoor dining area? Or perhaps a sheltered sun-trap, south-facing in the northern hemisphere, to extend the sitting-out season in a cooler climate? If space permits, you may want seating in both sun and shade. A seat should always have a good view, and will itself constitute part of the view from elsewhere. It will probably form a focal point from some other part of the garden, so site it with this in mind. Surround it with aromatic herbs, in containers if necessary. Choose herbs which release their perfume when touched, and plant them within hand's reach.

as a sculpture or sundial, can provide a focal point or lead the eye further into the garden, tempting the visitor to explore.

Victorian cloches and terracotta rhubarb forcers have become almost commonplace now, but nevertheless remain attractive objects in their own right. Wine-makers' glass demijohns make lovely cloches if you can find a glass-cutter brave enough to remove the base. It is a tricky operation and you must expect a high failure rate, but they are so inexpensive it is worth trying.

If painted furniture or objects are used in the garden, darker colours in misty shades of blue, grey or green blend better with plants than do paler colours. Although often chosen, white stands out quite starkly, an effect which is not always desirable. Select materials and colours that complement both the hard landscaping and the planting.

The choice of material for free-standing seats poses a dilemma. Plastic generally looks unsatisfactory. Wood, stone and metal blend more harmoniously into the garden scene, but are more expensive and likely to require maintenance. Wood is more comfortable to sit on than metal or stone, which can be either too cold or too hot unless cushioned. A free-standing seat intended as a permanent feature should look reasonably substantial. Anything flimsy can lend an unsettling aura of impermanence.

Walled medieval herb gardens often had seating incorporated into a raised bed which went round the entire perimeter of the garden. This must have been delightful, bringing the sitter into close proximity to the plants. Why not plant a camomile seat as part of a raised bed? It could be given distinct boundaries with a pair of topiary 'sofa arms' on either side.

The earth under the seat should be very slightly raised above the level of the retaining wall to allow the camomile to grow over the wall and provide padding for the edge of the seat. For comfort and safety, choose a smooth material such as brick for the low wall. Follow the instructions on page 50 for planting camomile lawns and seats.

SUNDIALS AND SCULPTURE

Sundials have been used for centuries as centrepieces for herb gardens. Traditionally they served a spiritual as well as a practical purpose in reminding the garden visitor of the passing of time and their own mortality, and were often inscribed with a philosophical adage to this effect. If chosen with care, sculpture or statues do not look out of place in the herb garden. The scale of the chosen feature is critical – too big and it will be overpowering, too small and it may lack the desired impact. It is difficult to visualize the final effect out of context, so try

A camomile sofa with topiary box arms is the ideal seating for a herb garden. Plant aromatic herbs within touching distance.

out canes of varying size in the intended site. An ornament deserves a setting which shows it off to full advantage. A hedge or wall niche, or a central axial location, is often used to good effect, particularly when outdoor lighting is also installed, but statuary can also surprise and charm in a more informal setting of lush foliage.

WATER FEATURES

Water brings an extra dimension to the herb garden. A still pool can enhance a quiet contemplative atmosphere, and the sparkle of a fountain adds movement, sound and life. In most herb gardens a formal water feature is more suitable than an informal one. Site it in a sheltered position away from over-hanging trees or deciduous shrubs – dead leaves in the water are unsightly and release gases which are toxic to fish.

Where noise is a problem, the sound of running water can block it quite effectively, although getting the volume right is a fine balancing act. Rills – narrow, gently sloping water chan-nels with straight edges, usually linking formal pools – can be used in gardens where a naturalistic water feature would be out of place. If lack of space precludes a pool or rill, perhaps you could include water in the vertical plane, in the form of a wall fountain or spout, given a conveniently situated wall.

A raised pool can have a wide, flat coping that doubles as informal seating. In a garden used by children, safety is para-mount, and any water feature should have some means of escape for pets or small wild animals which may fall in.

DECORATIVE PLANT SUPPORTS

The range of decorative plant supports has increased drama-tically in recent years. Metal obelisks are now ubiquitous, and 'umbrella frames', like those first used by Monet at Giverny, are marketed by mail order. The small ads in the back of gar-dening magazines usually offer a considerable choice of plant supports, and it can be surprisingly inexpensive to commis-sion custom-made ironwork from a blacksmith.

Ornamental trellis obelisks can be purchased or even made without too much difficulty, and topped with a finial.

ABOVE: *For maximum colour intensity, lavender hedges are best viewed end-on. Grey stone makes the perfect partner.*
OPPOSITE: *The elegant formality of the planters and seat makes a pleasing contrast to the exuberant planting.*

They should be treated with a garden wood preservative and can be painted or stained to tone with other garden features: seats, railings, and so on. Since any wood in the garden will need regular maintenance to keep it in good condition, it is sensible to plant the obelisks with climbers that do not stay permanently attached, such as annuals, herbaceous climbers which die down completely in winter, or perennials which require hard annual pruning, so that the trellis will be accessi-ble for treatment at some point during the year.

Ornamental features made from plant materials, such as hazel or willow branches, can look very effective. Tall willow plant supports for climbing herbs such as hops can add instant, inexpensive height and structure to a new garden, but if making your own, be sure to remove the bark, otherwise your plant support may take root!

PLANTING THE HERB GARDEN

ONCE THE BASICS OF PLANNING AND DESIGNING THE HERB GARDEN HAVE BEEN TAKEN CARE OF, AND THE BACKBONE OF THE GARDEN IS IN PLACE, IT IS TIME TO THINK OF THE PRACTICAL AND AESTHETIC CONSIDERATIONS OF PLANTING YOUR GARDEN. NO MATTER WHAT STYLE OF HERB GARDENING YOU CHOOSE, IT IS ESSENTIAL TO UNDERSTAND THE PRINCIPLES OF COMBINING PLANT COLOURS, SHAPES AND TEXTURES. BY CAREFULLY CHOOSING PLANTS, AND TREATING THEM CORRECTLY, YOU CAN MAKE USE OF THE DECORATIVE QUALITIES OF HERBS TO ENHANCE YOUR GARDEN, WHETHER IT HAPPENS TO BE A LARGE FORMAL ONE OR SIMPLY A WINDOWBOX.

Fennel and delphiniums in the herb border at Barnsley House, Gloucestershire, England.

Designing with Herbs

Planting design for a herb garden is really very similar to planting design for any other ornamental garden. The plants must be grouped in pleasing combinations, taking into account their growing requirements. If you are not familiar with herbs, do some reading and visit established herb gardens at different times of year, taking notes and photographs. Seeing the herbs growing in a garden setting will give you more information than looking at young plants in a nursery. Spend time in your intended garden to get a real feel for the place. Planting inspiration often comes gradually, as a result of a familiarity with the site which is only acquired over time.

If your herb garden is attached to an old house, you may wish to design a planting with an appropriate period feel, perhaps restricting your choice of herbs to those that were in cultivation when the house was built. In this case, consult specialist garden history literature and societies.

Is is a good idea to make a rough planting plan, drawn more or less to scale, marking the positions of key plants. These are evergreens and deciduous shrubs that will form the structural backbone of the garden, and any statuesque, architectural herbaceous plants which will predominate during the summer months. Smaller plants do not necessarily need their positions plotted, but can be arranged in the garden at planting time.

HERBS AND THEIR HABITATS

For healthy, well-grown herbs which are a pleasure to look at and to use, it is crucial to match the requirements of each plant to its site. The more you satisfy a plant's specific needs, the better it will grow and the more at home it will look in its setting. Generally it involves less work to select herbs for the conditions you have available than to attempt to alter those conditions. Where herbs are to be close neighbours, choose plants with similar or compatible growing requirements. In a herb garden it may be tempting to group them according to function, but do this only if you can also meet each plant's needs, or the results will be disappointing.

Try to match neighbouring plants in vigour. Some herbs are very energetic – turn your back for an instant and they take over the garden. If you put slower-growing, more delicate plants in their vicinity, the latter will not stand a chance. Unless you are prepared constantly to play the role of referee, it is as well to do one of the following: put all the invaders in the same area and let them fight it out; avoid them altogether; or take steps to confine their spread such as keeping them in large pots, which can be sunk to the rim in the herb garden.

OPPOSITE: *Golden variegated lemon balm, blue bugle and white woodruff provide ample contrast in both colour and form.*
ABOVE: *In this grouping lavender, tricolor sage and golden feverfew are enlivened by the sharp red of opium poppies.*

PLANT ASSOCIATIONS

When planning plant associations, try to achieve a balance between evergreen and herbaceous plants. A good winter backbone of evergreens is useful, but the growth and change provided by herbaceous elements will add dynamic interest. Place herbaceous plants in a position where the gap they leave in winter will not detract too much from the overall picture. Unless they are striking enough to stand alone, place plants in groups to avoid a bitty appearance. Tradition has it that odd numbers make better groups for planting than even numbers. The recurrence of selected key plants at intervals within the wider planting can be a useful device. It adds a feeling of rhythm and unity to the design, and gives a sense of purpose to the planting scheme.

Structure is important, and some plants are definitely more structural than others – many herbs are rather loose and sprawling in habit. Start with a good framework of bold, architectural plants – topiary, standard honeysuckles, lollipop bay trees, tall umbellifers such as fennel and lovage – to provide elements of drama within the planting, then fill in with the less flamboyant contenders.

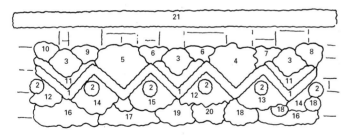

A formal herb border for a shady site, backed by a tall yew hedge. The taller plants at the back of the border are contained by a 90cm (3ft) high zig-zag of clipped box, and height is provided by blue-painted obelisks planted with golden hops. Lollipops of clipped bay punctuate the design, and the stone paving is both practical and attractive. Mints are planted in buried pots to prevent them spreading.

PLANT LIST
1. *Buxus sempervirens*
2. *Laurus nobilis*
3. *Humulus lupulus* 'Aureus'
4. *Angelica archangelica*
5. *Levisticum officinale*
6. *Symphytum* × *uplandicum* 'Variegatum'
7. *Melissa officinalis* 'Aurea'
8. *Mentha spicata* 'Moroccan'
9. *Mentha* × *piperata*
10. *Mentha* × *gracilis*
11. *Polygonatum multiflorum*
12. *Iris versicolor*
13. *Myrrhis odorata*
14. *Filipendula ulmaria* 'Aurea'
15. *Filipendula ulmaria* 'Variegata'
16. *Galium odoratum*
17. *Petroselinum crispum*
18. *Allium shoenoprasum*
19. *Coriandrum sativum*
20. *Anthriscus cerefolium*
21. *Taxus baccata*

Contrasts, whether of growth habit, leaf or flower shape, colour or texture have the effect of accentuating the characteristics that are juxtaposed. Spiky tree onions (*Allium cepa* Proliferum Group) look so much more spiky behind soft mounds of golden feverfew (*Tanacetum parthenium* 'Aureum') than when growing in isolation. The glaucous tree onion foliage also makes a good colour contrast with the yellow of feverfew. One contrast which is always effective is that of clipped with loose. The discipline of clipped hedges anchors softer plantings, and increases the feeling of abundance.

It is, however, possible to overdo contrast. If every plant in a border is in stark contrast to its neighbour, the effect is disjointed, rather than harmonious. Pale flowers or seedheads may well show up best against a dark background, but will look equally attractive merging into a gentle haze. Contrast is important in a garden, but use it with moderation, balanced by restful areas of harmonious blending.

At the planning stage think about whether the planting will be seen most often from a distance or in close-up. The contrasting of leaf shapes is generally only effective at a close range unless the leaves are particularly large. Contrasting flower shapes and colours are generally visible from further away, since they tend to stand out against the less differentiated background of foliage. Effects which rely on the overall shape and growth habit of the plant will be longer-lasting than those which rely on flower shape.

Use the growth habit of herb plants to good effect. Choose low-growing floppers, such as lady's mantle (*Alchemilla mollis*), to soften the edge of a hard path or weave back into upright planting behind. Avoid too strict an adherence to a 'tall-at-the-back, short-at-the-front' style of border planting. Evenly sloping beds of plants can look monotonous.

The texture of foliage and flowers can be highly distinctive. Leaves and flowers may be matt or shiny, smooth or felted, hard, soft, veined, crinkled, opaque or translucent. Texture has a big impact on colour, influencing the way light is reflected or absorbed. Some leaves are covered in tiny hairs, which give them a velvety feel and a pale appearance, others have a shiny cuticle which may make them look darker or constantly wet. Texture alone can lend a sensual appeal which justifies the growing of certain herbs. Finely cut young tansy leaves have a ferny delicacy that compensates for the plant's slightly too insistent yellow flowers and invasive tendencies.

In the herb garden, interesting leaves are probably the single most important factor in putting together good plant associations. Flowers may be transient but leaves remain throughout the growing season, and sometimes through the winter. Early in the season new leaves emerge in all their perfection, small and pristine. As the year advances they grow, perhaps losing some of their initial freshness, but still changing, developing and adding to the garden picture.

Above: *The rosa mundi in full flower next to golden oregano makes a sparkling combination.*
Right: *Chives in flower, purple sage and variegated lemon balm are slightly a less dazzling combination, but still make a lovely association of form and foliage.*

COLOUR-THEMED PLANTING

Monochrome or two-tone herb plantings can look stunning in the right setting, but remember to take into account the colour of any hard-landscaping materials. The same golden oregano which looks lovely against grey stone can look dreadful next to red brick paving of the wrong shade.

Purple- or bronze-leaved herbs look wonderful with grey foliage, and if blue flowers can be added, so much the better. Dark bronze foliage, such as that of purple-leaved elder (*Sambucus nigra* 'Guincho Purple') also makes an excellent foil for the hotter flower colours of herbs such as nasturtiums (*Tropaeolum majus*) or *Lobelia cardinalis*.

Some grey-leaved herbs produce flowers of a strident yellow which overwhelms the pale foliage. If you choose a herb for its leaves but dislike the flowers, be ruthless and cut them off. This can also enhance the quality of the foliage.

The combination of yellow leaves with variegated yellow and plain green leaves is pleasing – and any plant with blue, yellow or white flowers will complement this sort of scheme. Exercise restraint though, as too many variegated plants together can be overpowering. Green is, after all, the basic colour of plant life, and is soothing on the eye. A scheme of grey foliage with flowers in white or pastel shades is restful, and likely to be suitable for a hot, dry site.

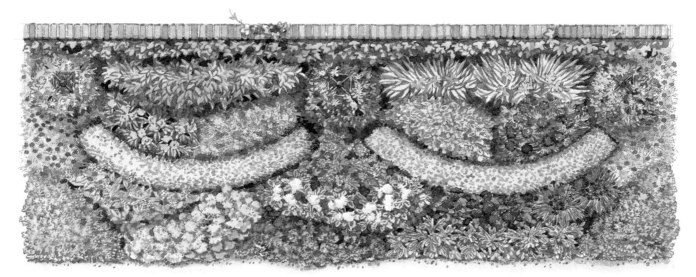

This yellow-themed herb border incorporates clipped ellipses of Lonicera nitida *'Baggesen's Gold' and tall willow plant supports to give height and structure to the planting.*

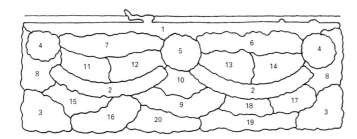

PLANT LIST
1. *Humulus lupulus* 'Aureus'
2. *Lonicera nitida* 'Baggesen's Gold'
3. *Oreganum vulgare* 'Aureum'
4. *Lonicera japonica* 'Aureoreticulata'
5. *Lonicera periclymenum* 'Graham Thomas'
6. *Iris pseudacorus* 'Variegata'
7. *Sambucus nigra* 'Plumosa Aurea'
8. *Nigella damascena* 'Miss Jekyll'
9. *Filipendula ulmaria* 'Aurea'
10. *Tanacetum vulgare* var. *crispum*
11. *Oenothera biennis*
12. *Foeniculum vulgare*
13. *Melissa officinalis* 'Aurea'
14. *Aconitum napellus*
15. *Borago officinalis*
16. *Alchemilla mollis*
17. *Allium schoenoprasum* var. *sibiricum*
18. *Heliotropium* 'Marine'
19. *Salvia officinalis* 'Icterina'
20. *Petroselinum crispum* (moss-curled)

This bronze and grey planting for a warm, sunny wall makes use of contrasting foliage. The brick and cobble paths radiating from the centre to facilitate herb harvesting and maintenance.

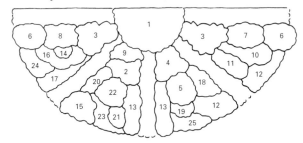

PLANT LIST
1. *Sambucus nigra* 'Guincho Purple'
2. *Artemisia* 'Powis Castle'
3. *Verbascum thapsus*
4. *Foeniculum vulgare* 'Purpureum'
5. *Tanacetum balsamita tomentosum*
6. *Santolina pinnata* ssp. *neapolitana*
7. *Eupatorium purpureum* ssp. *maculatum* 'Atropurpureum'
8. *Atriplex hortensis* var. *rubra*
9. *Angelica gigas*
10. *Artemisia abrotanum*
11. *Lavandula stoechas* ssp. *pedunculata*
12. *Ajuga reptans* 'Catlin's Giant'
13. *Nepeta racemosa*
14. *Allium cepa* Proliferum Group
15. *Sempervivum tectorum*
16. *Santolina chamaecyparissus*
17. *Ajuga reptans* 'Burgundy Glow'
18. *Salvia officinalis* Purpurascens Group
19. *Allium fistulosum*
20. *Thymus* 'Silver Posie'
21. *Ruta graveolens* 'Jackman's Blue'
22. *Salvia lavandulifolia*
23. *Ajuga reptans* 'Atropurpurea'
24. *Salvia officinalis* 'Tricolor'
25. *Rumex sanguineus*

Experiment with colour groupings while your new herb plants are still in their pots, moving them around until you find the right combination. Plants themselves can vary considerably in their flower and leaf colour, depending on the conditions in which they are grown. Most gardening books tell you not to move plants when they are in full leaf, but as long as they are well watered before and after moving, and lifted with a large enough rootball, most plants can be moved when in active growth. If a plant is very leafy, or the weather is hot, cut back some of the foliage to minimize water stress.

A planting scheme of pink and purple roses and salvias makes a harmonious combination in these box-edged beds.

PLANTING FOR SCENT AND SOUND

Scented plants should be situated where they will be appreciated most, along the edge of a path, or near a bench. Their perfume often seems to gain in intensity when they are grown in a warm, sheltered area, such as an enclosed terrace or patio. While some are undoubtedly beautiful, scented herbs are not always the most glamorous of plants, so place them among more attractive ones to get the best of both worlds. When selecting cultivars of herbs such as lavender, check that the improved appearance of the plant has not been achieved at the expense of perfume. Some herbs do not release their perfume until the leaves are crushed or rubbed. Site these next to the path, where they provide a sensory frisson in passing.

Sound can come from the plants themselves, perhaps rustling in a gentle breeze, or, more likely in a herb garden, from the many pollinating insects and songbirds which are attracted to them. Even without trying, the mere fact of cultivating a wide range of herbs in the garden is sure to bring in a variety of birds and insects.

EXTENDING THE SEASON

Some of the more commonly grown herbs have quite a short season, so it is worth seeking out those which either start early or go on late, to extend the season. Sweet cicely, sweet woodruff, bugle, chives, primroses, cowslips, fennel, feverfew, golden hops, lungwort, myrtle, pasque flower and lily-of-the-valley are all good early in the year. Plants which perform well later in the season include acanthus, bugbane, camphor, castor oil plant, golden rod, hyssop, Joe Pye weed, marsh mallow, pokeweed, wintergreen and witch hazel. Some of the faster-growing annual herbs will perform over an extended period if successional seed sowings are made.

Planting Practicalities

With the hard landscaping completed and planting plans drawn up, it is now almost time to think about planting some herbs, but first the soil must be in a fit state to receive them. Time and effort spent on soil preparation will be repaid several times over during the subsequent life of the garden, so try not to be in too much of a hurry to start planting.

PREPARING THE GROUND

Ideally, preparation should be timed so that planting can take place in spring, allowing a full growing season for perennial herbs to become established before they have to face the winter. However, with container-grown herbs planting can be done at any time in the growing season. If the summer has been hot and dry, early autumn is a good time to plant, since the herbs will not be subjected to the stress of drought and will have time to make good root growth before winter.

Clear the area thoroughly of both perennial and annual weeds before planting takes place. It is impossible to remove every single weed, but aim to get rid of as many as possible at the outset, especially the pernicious spreaders such as couch grass, bindweed and ground elder. If the planting area is not very large, it can be cleared by thorough digging and removal of weed root fragments. In practice some bits of root will inevitably escape and regrow, requiring attention later. Expect to spend small but regular amounts of time on weed control throughout each growing season. Where a large area needs clearing, particularly when persistent perennial weeds are present, various labour-saving techniques can be used. A

RIGHT: *A planting scheme does not have to be complicated to be effective. This sea of hazy* Nigella damascena *enclosed by clipped box needs no improvement.*
OPPOSITE: *The feathery green foliage of fennel, combined with accents of red and orange, forms an insubstantial screen that invites a peek through, rather than blocking the view.*

reliable organic method of clearing weedy ground involves covering it with a light-excluding material such as black plastic or old carpet, and waiting for the weeds to die. This is a cheap and environmentally safe method, but patience is required. With a few of the worst perennial weeds it can take up to two full growing seasons, but for most one season is sufficient. For faster results, a non-residual weedkiller such as glyphosate may be used, but where herbs are to be grown for medicinal purposes, I would not recommend this. If empty beds are too much to bear, using chemicals for the initial clearance but not cropping any herbs in the first year might be an acceptable compromise

Before planting can take place, cultivation is necessary, to allow air, water and roots to penetrate the soil. Starting at one end of the bed, dig the soil over systematically in trenches to the depth of one spit (a spade's depth), piling the soil from the first trench into a wheelbarrow. Fork over the bottom of the trench, breaking up any hard, compacted soil so that water

can drain away and roots penetrate easily. Pile the soil from the second trench into the empty adjacent trench, and so on, using the soil from the barrow to fill the last trench.

Most soils will benefit from the addition of bulky organic material, such as garden compost or well-rotted manure, which improves moisture retention, aeration and drainage. This can be forked into the soil during or after digging. If the soil is heavy and badly drained, coarse gravel can be added to help open it up. Dry, pelleted poultry manure is a good fertilizer for poor, exhausted soil, but use it as a supplement – do not omit the organic material. This will enable you to grow the more leafy green herbs, but many of the aromatic herbs, particularly those with grey or silver leaves, thrive in poor, well-drained soil. If this is the type of soil you have, leave some of it less enriched to enable you to grow them successfully.

HEDGES AND KNOTS

If hedges, knots or parterres are included in the design, plant them first. Prepare the site well beforehand, adding slow-release high-phosphate organic fertilizer, such as rock phosphate, to the soil to promote rapid root growth and establishment.

Container-grown hedging plants can be planted at almost any time of year provided the weather is not too cold. Bare-rooted or root-balled plants are a cheaper alternative, but should be planted at the times recommended in the chart.

Planting should take place as soon as the hedging plants have been obtained. Water them thoroughly, and leave bare-rooted plants to soak for an hour or so before planting. Mark out the planting lines and dig the holes, or a trench if the planting distance is less than 45cm (18in). The easiest way to mark straight lines is to stretch garden line between two pegs.

HEDGING AND KNOT PLANTS

	Soil Type	Spacing	Planting Time	When to clip	
TALLER HEDGES				*During growth*	*Fully grown*
Yew *(Taxus baccata)*	Well-drained soils, dislikes pollution	50cm (20in)	Mid to late spring	Midsummer, then every six weeks	Late summer
Beech *(Fagus sylvatica)*	Most well-drained soils, including chalk	45cm (18in)	Autumn to early spring	Late summer	Late summer
Hornbeam *(Carpinus)*	Most well-drained soils	45cm (18in)	Autumn to early spring	Late summer	Late summer
Privet *(Ligustrum)*	Most soils	30cm (12in)	Autumn to spring	Midsummer, then every six weeks	Late spring
LOW HEDGES FOR KNOTS AND PARTERRES					
Dwarf box *(Buxus sempervirens 'Suffruticosa')*	Well-drained soils including chalk	15cm (6in)	Mid to late spring	Midsummer, then every six weeks	Late summer
Cotton lavender *(Santolina)*	Most well-drained soils	20cm (8in)	Spring to autumn (container-grown plants only)	Midsummer to late summer, every six weeks	Midsummer to late summer, every six weeks
Wall germander *(Teucrium x lucidrys)*	Well-drained, slightly alkaline soil	15cm (6in)	Spring to autumn (container-grown plants only)	Late spring to autumn, every six weeks	Spring and autumn

To mark circles or curves, fix one peg in the ground and, keeping the line taut with the second peg attached to it, make a groove in the soil. The curve can be made more obvious by trickling sand along it.

Plants should be planted to the depth at which they were grown in the nursery. With bare-rooted plants a soil mark will be visible on the stem. Remove pot-grown plants from their containers. If the roots were circling the base of the pot, spread them out carefully and trim with sharp, clean secateurs. Place the plant in the hole, which should accommodate the rootball easily, adjusting the height if necessary. Fill the hole with soil, firming it in by treading gently on it as you go. On windy sites, staking may be necessary.

The hedge must be kept well watered in its first season. A mulch of compost or bark chips, applied when the soil is wet, will conserve moisture. Regular feeding is also necessary for optimum growth during the early life of a hedge. An annual

OPPOSITE: *Rhubarb left to flower adds a touch of drama to this otherwise controlled herb garden scene.*
RIGHT: *Frequent trimming keeps this skirt of golden marjoram* (Origanum vulgare *'Aureum') neat and compact.*

ABOVE: *Orange marigolds with blue borage flowers. The strong contrast makes the colours seem even more intense.*
OPPOSITE: *Dense herb planting produces a weed-suppressing canopy of foliage – this is ground-cover at its most exciting.*

application of rock phosphate around its base, followed by pelleted chicken manure, and/or a mulch of well-rotted manure or garden compost, will all help.

The initial pruning and training is vital in making a dense, bushy hedge. In terms of shape, it should be wider at the base than at the top, to allow light to reach the lower branches. Deciduous hedging plants that have a bushy growth habit (beech, hornbeam) should have their leaders (the main, upright shoot) cut back by a third at the time of planting. Cut back the stronger lateral branches by a third of their length and, in the second winter, cut them back by a third of the previous season's growth. Box is also treated in this manner.

Deciduous plants that tend to grow tall and upright, such as privet, should be pruned more drastically on planting, to a height of 15cm (6in), then in the second year cut back quite hard again, leaving about 15cm (6in) of the previous season's growth. Evergreens (yew and most conifers) have the leader left unpruned until the desired height is reached. Trim the lateral shoots to encourage bushy growth.

HERBS

With your planting plan to hand, start by positioning the key plants, still in their pots, in their approximate locations. Take a good look at them from various places in the garden, checking the sight lines from significant locations such as seats, house windows, paths and gateways. When planting small specimens which will grow tall, it may help to insert canes of an appropriate height at the intended planting places. Sometimes problems overlooked at the design stage become obvious when planting, or you may have flashes of inspiration.

Plant only when you are satisfied with the positioning of all the key plants. With the basic framework in place, repeat the process using first the medium-sized and finally the smaller fill-in plants. Container-grown plants need to be well watered before they are planted. Remove plants from their pots just before planting and examine the roots. If they are circling the base of the pot, untangle them gently and trim them, to encourage them to branch. Dig a planting hole large enough to accommodate the plant with ease, and place the plant in the hole so that the soil comes to the level it was at in the pot. Gently firm the soil around the plant to eliminate air pockets.

WATERING

Water the newly planted garden regularly in the first growing season. Newly planted herbs should never be allowed to wilt – coping with life out of a pot is quite enough stress for them to experience at any one time. Some plants, particularly evergreens, will not show any immediate signs of dehydration, even though they can be badly damaged or killed by it, so be especially vigilant where these are concerned.

HERB PROPAGATION

Propagating herbs is generally quite a straightforward process, whether they are grown from seed or raised from cuttings, and it makes sense, if you have the time and space, to raise as many as possible yourself. Named cultivars usually need to be propagated from cuttings or division, as they are hybrids or sports and will not breed true from seed.

Sowing seeds Sow seeds in module trays or small pots in spring, indoors. Fill the containers lightly with a proprietary seed compost, and tap them sharply downwards on a flat surface to settle the compost. Water with tap water, so that the compost is uniformly moist and sow the seeds thinly on the surface. Fine seed may be mixed with dry sand to enable it to be sown thinly enough. Place the trays or pots on a well-lit windowsill out of direct sunlight.

Some seeds need light to germinate, a few need total darkness, the majority are not fussy. The first should be covered with a thin layer of horticultural grit, which admits light but keeps the seeds in contact with the compost. The rest may be covered with a thicker layer of grit or sieved compost, usually to the depth of the seed. The compost should be kept moist until germination occurs. Use a propagator, or place a cut-off plastic drinks bottle or a plastic bag over the pot to maintain a humid environment, gradually reducing the humidity after germination. Water using a hand-held misting spray.

Give the seedlings room to grow. They can be gradually thinned, using tweezers if necessary, when still very tiny. Multiple seedlings in pots may need transitional pricking out into individual pots, and growing on until large enough to cope outside. If using modules, gradually thin the seedlings to one per module and plant out when the roots fill the space, after all danger of frost has passed. Before planting out, seedlings should be hardened off over a two-week period, exposing them to outdoor life for lengthening periods, but protecting them if the weather turns cold and taking them in at night. Water seedlings well before planting out. If the roots have circled around the base of the pot they may need to be disentangled and trimmed back cleanly before planting out.

Direct sowing When sowing seed in the ground in spring, wait for the soil to warm up. If you sow too early the results will be disappointing. Soil-warming can be hastened by covering the ground with black plastic or cloches a couple of weeks before sowing. The seed-bed must be well cultivated, and the soil broken up to a fine tilth, clear of weeds and large stones. On very heavy soils, take out shallow drills and line them with seed compost. The same principles apply whether sowing in a separate seed-bed for subsequent transplanting, or sowing seed directly where it is to grow. Sow in rows so

Opposite above: *Careful choice of planting position results in a rewarding mix of colour, shape and texture.*
Opposite below: *Feverfew* (Tanacetum parthenium), *and pot marigolds* (Calendula officinalis), *are both easy to raise from seed.*
Above: *Camomile paths intersect this charming herb garden. Lawn camomile is propagated by dividing the offsets in spring.*

that the seedlings are easily differentiated from weeds. As the seedlings grow, thin them to the correct spacing so the rows join up and cease to be obvious.

Cuttings There are various types of cuttings, and some herbs are more amenable to propagation by one method than another. Softwood cuttings are usually taken in late spring or early summer, from the new growth before it has hardened at all. Semi-ripe cuttings are taken at a slightly later stage, when the current season's new growth has started to harden at the base. Softwood and semi-ripe cuttings should be 10–18cm (4–7in) long. Deciduous hardwood cuttings can be used to propagate a limited number of woody herbs, and require the minimum of aftercare. They are taken after leaf-fall in the autumn, or a few weeks prior to bud-break in early spring. They should be 20–30cm (8–12in) long.

Collect propagation material early in the morning, while the parent plants are still fresh after the cool of the night. Use a sharp knife, or a pair of secateurs, to slice just below a leaf node. If the plant has long interlodes, the cut can be made midway between nodes. Remove the lower leaves and insert the cutting gently into the compost, just deep enough to hold it upright. If you cannot do this immediately, wrap the cutting in polythene and refrigerate it until you are ready to deal with it. Use a free-draining cutting compost – if you intend to much propagation, you can mix your own by combining half and half peat and fine-grade chipped bark by volume.

Place softwood and semi-ripe cuttings in a warm, shaded, humid environment. A good method is to place the pot of cuttings on a saucer of wet gravel on a shady indoor windowsill. Cover the pot with a large plastic drinks bottle which has had its base cut off. Leave the screw top in place for the first few days, and keep the saucer topped up with water. Ventilate gradually by removing the screw top, but put it back immediately if the cuttings show signs of wilting.

Hardwood cuttings can be kept in a greenhouse or in a coldframe, without covering, or can be rooted directly into trenches in the garden. Water quite sparingly, until there are signs of growth in spring.

Plant division Many clump-forming herbs can be propagated by division, in autumn or spring. If there are a lot of leaves still on the plant, cut them back quite hard, but leave some new growth, if there is any, as this will provide nutrients for the new plants. Dig up the clump and either tease the roots apart or cut the clump into pieces with a clean sharp knife, discarding the woody central part. Rinsing the soil from the rootball often makes the clump fall apart quite easily. If the plant is too large to dig up in its entirety, it is usually possible to clear the soil away from the side and cut off some of the newer growth. Pot or replant the divisions without delay.

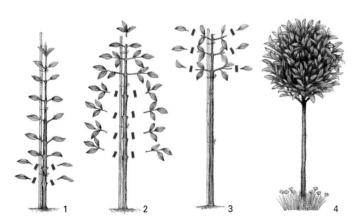

1. While the plant is still small, tie the developing shoot to a cane, making sure not to crush it.

2. Remove the lower leaves and side shoots very gradually, as the main shoot grows.

3. When the desired height is reached, cut off the growing point cleanly. Allow side shoots to develop around the crown, but keep pinching out their growing points to promote branching, which will produce a dense head.

4. Gradually clip the head into a globe, removing any unwanted shoots from the stem when they are still small. Keep in shape by trimming regularly.

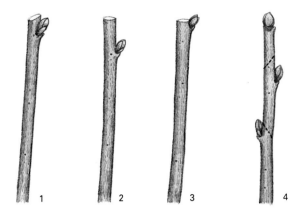

1. A correct pruning cut, just above, and sloping away from the bud, so as to allow rain water to drain away from the bud.
2. The cut is too far from the bud, and the stem will die back as a result.
3. The cut is too close to the bud, and may well have damaged it.
4. Note the direction of the cut in relation to the position of the buds.

ABOVE: *These apple trees are being trained as espaliers, with careful pruning and tying in of young branches.*
OPPOSITE BELOW: *A miniature box tree trained as a standard punctuates an expanse of closely clipped lavender.*

TOPIARY AND STANDARDS

Producing topiary is a long-term project. The plants most often used are slow-growing, which is an advantage once the desired shape has been achieved, as an annual trim will keep them looking neat. Box and yew shapes will take about five years to start looking good. If speed is of the essence, ivy (*Hedera helix*) can be trained on to wire frames, or one of the faster-growing plants, such as privet (*Ligustrum*) or *Lonicera nitida*, can be used, but subsequent maintenance will be more time-consuming as they will need more frequent clipping.

Simple shapes can be formed by clipping freehand, but anything complicated will need a frame. Green-painted wire frames are available commercially, or make your own, using canes, galvanized wire, and wire netting.

To clip cones and obelisks accurately, make a cutting guide from canes wired together. In the early stages, topiary should be clipped quite frequently, about every six weeks throughout the growing season, as little and often promotes maximum growth. When mature, an annual clipping is enough for most genera. As a general principle it is inadvisable to remove all of the previous year's growth.

If growing topiary in containers, repot the plants annually, and make sure the container is large enough, as the top will not grow if the roots are too cramped. Pruning the thicker roots when re-potting will encourage the growth of fine feeder roots. Continue to feed even when plants reach the desired size, as this will help maintain a dense covering of leaves.

Some herbs, including bay, rosemary, honeysuckle, and some of the scented pelargoniums, can be trained as standard (see opposite). With the exception of bay, these herbs will need a permanent stake to keep them upright.

PRUNING AND TRAINING

Pruning is often necessary, both to produce herb plants of the shape and size desired, and to encourage the growth of new foliage and flowers for harvesting.

To stimulate a plant into producing lots of bushy lateral growth, it is generally best to prune it quite hard at the onset of its natural growing period. As a general principle, the more of a plant you cut off, the faster and more vigorous will be the regrowth, although you can take this too far. Hard pruning is always a shock to the plant, so it should be fed and given the best possible growing conditions to help it recover. If tender or borderline plants are pruned when there is still danger of frost, they can be damaged, or even die as a result. They are generally best pruned in late spring or early summer.

Most woody herbs benefit from some formative pruning to make them bush out, and even some of the softer herbaceous plants should be treated this way. With many plants this will have been done at the nursery, but if a new plant is straggly, trim it when planting out, and keep pinching out the growing tips to make it branch. When pruning woody herbs the pruning cut should slope away from the bud (see page 49).

Climbers, such as golden hops or honeysuckles, can be trained up ornamental supports made of wood or metal. Plenty of designs are available commercially, but do ensure that the frame is strong enough for the plant selected.

CAMOMILE LAWNS AND SEATS

Unless you adore weeding, do not be tempted to make a camomile lawn very large. It will always need regular hand-weeding, although you will only have to mow it about once a year. A seat in a raised bed is probably a more practical alternative for most people.

The site must be sunny and the soil well drained to ensure success. Do not plant in an area that will receive a lot of traffic, as camomile will not cope with the same wear and tear as grass. Level the site with repeated raking and remove all large stones. Use *Chamaemelum nobile* 'Treneague', a non-flowering, very low-growing clone, planted about 10–15cm (4–6in) apart. In the first season, do not allow anyone to walk or sit on it for at least three months, and shear lightly at regular intervals to promote branching. Water regularly.

Every spring, collect spare offsets from areas where there are too many and use them to fill any gaps that have appeared. Apply liquid feed at intervals through the growing season, or scatter pelleted chicken manure early in the season.

ABOVE: *Bark chips laid over a weed-proof lining make an informal, low-maintenance path.*
OPPOSITE: *A mixture of containers planted with an assortment of herbs makes a pleasing group on a sunny terrace.*

TREES IN THE HERB GARDEN

There are a variety of smaller trees, or trees which can be kept small by pruning, suitable for herb gardens, most of which are used medicinally.

Both the pink apothecary's rose (*Rosa gallica* var. *officinalis*) and its pink-and-white striped sport, the rosa mundi (*Rosa gallica* 'Versicolor'), can be obtained as standards, and go well in a formal herb garden. Bay, box, yew, juniper and holly are more orthodox candidates, probably best treated as topiary and kept in check by clipping. Elder (*Sambucus nigra)* is a good and unusual choice. There are bronze-leaved and yellow cut-leaved forms as well as the more common green, and they are beautiful in flower and fruit. They may require encouragement to form a tree rather than a shrub shape (see page 48).

Containers and Small Spaces

No matter how small an area your garden covers, even if it consists of a single windowbox, there are still plenty of ways of using that space to the full.

HERBS IN CONTAINERS

The majority of herbs adapt well to growing in containers but they need to be watered more frequently in dry weather than herbs grown in the ground. Small pots dry out rapidly in hot weather, making watering a constant chore, so select containers which are large enough to hold a reasonable volume of compost. Match the plant to the container – it can be just as bad to place a small plant in too large a container as the reverse, and as many plants are lost from over-watering as from drought. Generally, plants which enjoy dry conditions should be grown in smaller pots than those needing a more moist environment, and plants with abundant foliage lose water more rapidly than those with fewer leaves.

Herbs that cannot be grown successfully in pots are those which produce long tap roots or those which are simply too big, such as angelica and elecampane. Some herbs, such as members of the poppy family, have delicate roots and dislike being transplanted. Raise them in modules or individual pots

and plant out when still quite small, after a very thorough watering. Others, such as coriander, need a cool root run and tend to bolt (set seed prematurely) if grown in pots, where temperature fluctuations are more pronounced.

Container growing should not automatically be seen as second best to planting in the ground. Some of the more invasive herbs, such as the mints, are probably better confined to pots. There are also half-hardy herbs, such as lemon grass, the scented pelargoniums, lemon verbena, which can kept in pots and moved indoors for the winter in cooler climates.

The sun- and heat-loving plants should be grown in a free-draining compost in a sunny, sheltered position, while herbs needing shade and moisture can be stood in saucers of water and positioned to take advantage of shade from buildings, walls or nearby trees.

A windowbox of culinary herbs for a sunny site, planted with (left to right) Origanum vulgare 'Aureum', Anthriscus cerefolium, Allium shoenoprasum *var.* sibiricum, Petroselinum crispum, Laurus nobilis *and* Tropaeolum 'Alaska'.
Left: *Scented pelargoniums and purple-leaved sage sit happily in a handsome trough under an archway of old bricks.*

A container display is easier to manage if only one type of herb per pot is used. This permits maximum flexibility in bringing plants at their prime into the foreground, but there are other good practical reasons. Herbs differ in their vigour: more energetic genera can easily get out of hand, and some are even thought to produce root secretions that inhibit the growth of others. Where a short-term mixed planting in a single container is desired, select herbs of similar vigour and cultivation needs. The drought lovers are probably the safest option, since closely planted pots are more likely to dry out than to suffer from an excess of moisture.

If your only outdoor space is a windowsill, you can grow herbs in windowboxes. The boxes must be of sturdy construction, well secured, and reasonably deep (at least 20cm /8in, preferably more), with plenty of drainage holes. Cover the holes with crocks or pebbles to prevent the compost from washing out. Windowsills are often rather exposed, especially those above ground floor level, so before deciding which herbs to grow, monitor weather conditions for a while. The more delicate herbs, such as basil or tarragon, are unlikely to flourish without protection from harsh winds. Consider also how much direct sunlight the windowbox will receive, and choose your herbs accordingly. Windowboxes are likely to be in the rain shadow of the building, and if so may need to be watered even when heavy rain has fallen.

Few herbs will tolerate being frozen solid, so in regions where winters are cold, either protect windowboxes from frost and excessive rain by moving them into a greenhouse or conservatory, or treat them as temporary installations, starting afresh with new plants each spring.

Growing media for containers Herbs should be grown in a general-purpose potting compost, preferably organic. For perennial herbs to be grown for more than one season, mix two parts compost to one part coarse grit by volume to keep the compost open and assist drainage. Any plant grown in a pot for more than a season should be repotted annually in spring, and the compost replenished. Place a layer of crocks in the bottom before planting to prevent compost from washing out of the drainage holes.

Maintenance Small pots or those containing plants with a lot of leaf may need a thorough soaking more than once a day in summer. Keeping pots going all year round requires more care, since in cooler weather it is easy for them to become waterlogged, which can be very damaging. When herbs are not in active growth it is generally safer to keep all except

ABOVE: *Pot-grown topiary (*Lonicera nitida *'Baggesen's Gold') and a collection of tender mints, also in pots, can easily be moved under cover for winter protection.*
RIGHT: *Basil and scented-leaved pelargoniums are grown in an assortment of old olive oil cans and terracotta pots. The red pelargonium flowers pick up the colour of the well-used chair.*

those which are genuine bog plants quite dry perhaps by standing them in the rain-shadow of a wall, although they should never be allowed to wilt.

The more lush herbs grown in containers should either have a slow-release organic fertilizer mixed into the compost or applied as a top dressing in spring, or be fed regularly – about once a week – throughout the growing season with an organic liquid feed.

When herbs are in active growth, it is usually fine to trim them regularly. This happens as a matter of course when they are harvested, and most herbs regrow with no loss of vigour; indeed many seem to benefit. Container-grown herbs may need to be kept within bounds by regular trimming, particularly if a mixture of plants is grown in the same container. Some of the larger herbs, such as lovage, can be kept artificially small by frequent cutting, at least for the first year or two of their lives, without any apparent ill-effects, enabling them to be grown in a smaller space than is usually recommended. With plants like lovage which grow from the centre, harvest the outer leaves regularly, before they get too big and coarse.

TINY HERB GARDENS

Where space is very limited, it makes sense to avoid both the giants and those herbs which need to be grown in large quantities to be of use. Herbs with a long cropping season, such as chives, which can be cut and regrown repeatedly, or rosemary, which can be harvested year-round, might usefully be included, as might fast-growing annuals like nasturtiums, dill or borage. It is surprising how much can be grown in a relatively small area, especially if the bed is accessible from all sides, avoiding the need to walk on any potential growing space.

Rather than trying for some of everything, it might be better to concentrate on a theme, perhaps growing only culinary herbs, herbs for tea, medicinal or aromatic herbs, depending on individual preference, or even selecting herbs on the basis of foliage or flower colour. Using a single-colour theme is one way of bringing unity to a small space, and can result in a very appealing display.

Even in a very small space, ornamental features may be incorporated into the design, although it is important to get the scale right. Where ground space is really at a premium, do not neglect the vertical plane. Make full use of all available wall space to train climbing herbs such as hops or jasmine, or to attach containers. A narrow obelisk in the centre of a small herb bed can add the contrast of something hard and artificial, as well as providing a plant support for a climber. Use pots or topiary to add instant structure to a loose herb planting.

Part of the herb square shown opposite, in its first year. The box hedge plants will be more prominent in later years.

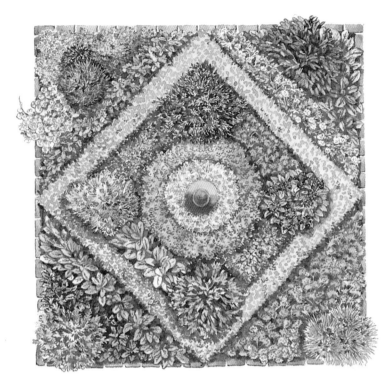

PLANT LIST
1. *Nigella damascena* 'Miss Jekyll'
2. *Origanum vulgare* 'Aureum'
3. *Rosmarinus officinalis* 'Miss Jessopp's Upright'
4. *Levisticum officinale*
5. *Artemisia abrotanum*
6. *Heliotropum* 'Marine'
7. *Thymus* 'Doone Valley'
8. *Rumex sanguineus*
9. *Petroselinum crispum hortense*
10. *Petroselinum crispum*
11. *Buxus sempervirens* 'Suffruticosa'
12. *Ruta graveolens* 'Jackman's Blue'
13. *Ocimum basilicum* 'Purple Ruffles'
14. *Rumex acetosa*
15. *Ocimum basilicum* 'Green Ruffles'
16. *Artemisia dracunculus*
17. *Thymus serpyllum* 'Russetings'
18. *Thymus* × *citriodorus*
19. *Tropaeolum majus* 'Alaska'
20. *Coriandrum sativum*
21. *Salvia officinalis* Purpurascens Group
22. *Allium schoenoprasum*
23. *Atriplex hortensis* var. *rubra*

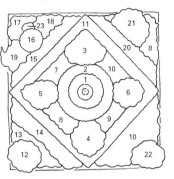

This bed of culinary herbs is only 1.5m (5ft) square, yet it produces a year-round supply. Herbs are planted closely, and frequent picking keeps them in their place.

BALCONIES AND ROOF GARDENS

The combined weight of plants, containers, moist compost, furniture and garden-users can be considerable, and before creating a herb garden on a balcony or roof it is essential to make sure that these structures will take the strain. If there is any doubt at all, seek professional advice. With roof gardens, try to position the heaviest items around the edges and directly over supporting walls.

Boundary walls or railings should be robust, and at least 1.1m (3ft 6in) in height, and railings should be close enough together to contain children or pets. All the herb containers and other heavy items, especially those near the edge of roofs, should be anchored securely. The fixings on some items, such as table parasols, while adequate for ground-level use, may not be strong enough for a windy roof or balcony,.

Balconies and roof gardens are often very exposed, and before any herb planting takes place provision must be made for shelter. Willow hurdles, trellis planted with climbers or even container-grown shrubs may be used, bearing in mind that it is better to slow the wind down than to create a solid barrier which can cause unpredictable air turbulence. Plan also to provide some shade, either with tall-growing plants or with some sort of artificial canopy or parasol.

It is important to have easy access for planting and maintenance, and for convenient watering it is useful to have an outside tap. For roof gardens the flooring surface should have a 1 in 60 fall, and some means of removing excess water, if only a slope leading to some external guttering. Water gulleys should not be sited in the corners, otherwise they will soon become blocked by fallen leaves.

Use expanded polystyrene rather than crocks for drainage in the base of containers, and peat or bark-based compost, not loam, for the sake of lightness, but make sure pots are not top-heavy as this makes them unstable. On a tiny balcony or roof garden, pots can be fixed securely to walls and railings to take advantage of every scrap of potential planting space.

HERB GARDEN PROFILES

THIS CHAPTER TAKES A DETAILED LOOK AT SOME DIVERSE HERB GARDENS, IN A VARIETY OF SETTINGS, URBAN AND RURAL, SHOWING HOW THE DESIGN PRINCIPLES AND TECHNIQUES ALREADY DISCUSSED HAVE BEEN PUT INTO PRACTICE. THE STYLES RANGE FROM THE MOST FORMAL OF CLIPPED PARTERRES TO THE MOST RELAXED OF COTTAGE GARDEN PLANTINGS. THE GARDENS VARY IN SIZE FROM A FEW SQUARE YARDS TO A THIRD OF AN ACRE, BUT THERE IS MUCH TO BE LEARNT FROM ALL OF THEM, AND IDEAS FROM THE LARGER GARDENS ARE EASILY ADAPTED TO SUIT A SMALLER SITE. ABOVE ALL, THIS CHAPTER IS ABOUT INSPIRATION, AND DEMONSTRATES THE EXTRAORDINARY VERSATILITY AND ADAPTABILITY OF HERBS AS ORNAMENTAL GARDEN PLANTS.

Espaliered fruit trees frame the herb garden at Hintlesham Hall, Suffolk, England.

Herbs in Mixed Borders

Judy's Country Garden at South Somercotes is part of Judy and Mike Harry's smallholding, situated in the Lincolnshire countryside only a short distance from the east coast of Britain. This part of the country is almost completely flat, and very exposed to sea gales, so providing shelter has been one of their main priorities. The garden is protected partly by walls, and partly by tree and shrub plantings. It has developed gradually over the past twenty years and continues to change, in a process of slow evolution, experimentation and expansion.

The style is cottagey, unpretentious and informal, in harmony with the house, a four-square brick-built smallholder's cottage which dates back to the nineteenth century. Relaxed planting spills abundantly over stone, grass and gravel paths, and plants are allowed to seed themselves with minimal intervention on the part of the gardener. Throughout the garden herbs are grown among the ornamental shrubs and perennials, grouped according to their preferred growing conditions. Good foliage herbs, such as rue, are often used at the front of a mixed border or to soften the edge of a path, and taller herbs are used to good effect as back-of-the-border plants.

The small, enticing plant nursery occupies the area to the west of the house, formerly the vegetable garden. It is very much a part of the garden as a whole – there is no factory-scale production here; seedlings nestle together in low cold frames, and the effect is more that of a gardener's enthusiasm run riot than of harsh commercialism. As Judy's garden expanded, so the nursery grew to accommodate new plant treasures, and the vegetables were gradually squeezed out.

Decorative features are understated, in keeping with the garden's informality, but there are a couple of well-placed

LEFT: *A buttress of clipped bay bulges out over the stone path. Herbs such as thyme and deadnettle have seeded between the paving stones.*
OPPOSITE: *Southernwood, fennel, thyme, lavender and oregano all enjoy the infertile soil, shelter and warmth near the south-facing wall of the house.*

garden seats, one sited for morning use, another for later in the day. Mike Harry made the attractive low wooden fences and gates which add to the cottagey atmosphere.

Both garden design and planting are informed by a sensitive awareness of plant ecology, and the desire to work with rather than against the prevailing conditions. Hence, those areas where the soil is rich and heavy were planted with the taller, more nutrient-hungry herbs, and the dry, poor soil next to the warm south-facing side of the house contains Mediterranean herbs which thrive on starvation rations.

LEFT: *Climbing roses in full bloom cover the walls of the house. Self-sown foxgloves echo the uprights of the fence posts, and red orach adds to the informal charm of this scene.*

BELOW: *This planting is an object lesson in matching plants of similar vigour. Rather than trying to control their natural excesses, the more invasive herbs, among them: red ink plant, motherwort, marsh-mallow, cardoons, curry plant, meadow cranesbill and fleabane, are simply grouped together in a large border and left to fight it out among themselves.*

OPPOSITE: *Poppies make a bold statement in a mixed border planting.*

KEY PLANTS
BEDS A
Allium fistulosum
Allium schoenoprasum
Allium tuberosum
Anthemis tinctoria
Artemisia absinthium
Claytonia sibirica
Hyssopus officinalis
Marrubium vulgare
Melissa officinalis 'Aurea'
Mentha spicata
Nepeta cataria
Rosa 'White Cockade'
Rumex scutatus
Ruta graveolens
Salvia lavandulifolia
Salvia officinalis Purpurascens
  Group
Saponaria officinalis 'Rosea Plena'
Tanacetum balsamita tomentosum
Teucrium chamaedrys
Thymus vulgaris aureus
Thymus vulgaris 'Silver Posie'
Verbena officinalis
Vitis vinifera 'Purpurea'
BEDS B
Allium cepa Proliferum Group
Anchusa officinalis
Artemisia abrotanum
Foeniculum vulgare
Foeniculum vulgare 'Purpureum'
Lamium maculatum 'White Nancy'
Laurus nobilis
Melissa officinalis 'All Gold'
Nepeta racemosa
Origanum vulgare
Phlomis fruticosa

Rosmarinus officinalis
Thymus pulegioides
BEDS C
Mixed planting
BED D
Lavandula 'Hidcote'
Santolina 'Edward Bowles'
Thymus 'Annie Hall'
Thymus 'Doone Valley'
Thymus 'Lemon Curd'
Thymus serpyllum 'Minimus'

1. Taxus baccata topiary

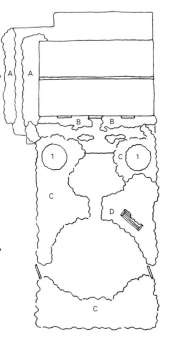

A Formal Herb Garden

Hintlesham Hall, near Ipswich in Suffolk, is a spectacular old mansion dating from the Elizabethan period, and is now a luxurious country house hotel. At the time the herb garden was made it was the home of Robert Carrier's cookery school. The garden was designed by the renowned plantswoman Beth Chatto to serve the cookery school, but these days it is used to supply the hotel restaurant and as a pleasure garden for the guests. This is a large herb garden, about one third of an acre, laid out as a living tapestry of parterres, but since it comprises a series of gardens within a garden, there are many ideas to adapt for a smaller site.

The ground plan of this garden is traditional and entirely appropriate to the grandeur of the house to which it is attached, but it is no mere historical reproduction. It was designed to keep maintenance to a minimum. Most of the individual herb beds are planted very simply, with just one type of herb in the centre and another around the edge, and so are relatively easy to look after, each type of plant being easily confined within its allotted space. The small herb beds are practical as well as pretty, in that they can be cultivated from the paths. A tall beech hedge with arched entrances, which borders the garden on two sides, provides both shelter and a sense of

seclusion. Two main grass paths lead from the hedge into the centre of the garden, and the many smaller paths among the herb beds are of gravel edged with cobbles. Both provide an excellent foil for the herb plants. The double row of ancient espaliered apple and pear trees marks the eastern boundary of the herb garden and acts as a formal division between it and the remains of an old orchard – a wilder, more informal area.

BELOW LEFT: *The willow* Salix caprea *'Kilmarnock' adds height to the otherwise low, cushion-like planting.*
BELOW RIGHT: *Artichokes, lavender, and a secluded bench make for a peaceful spot.*

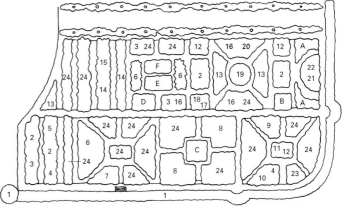

KEY PLANTS

BEDS A
Anthriscus cerefolium
Salvia officinalis
Salvia officinalis Purpurascens
 Group

BED B
Hyssopus officinalis ssp. *aristatus*
Laurus nobilis

BED C
Lavandula angustifolia
Lonicera nitida
Prunus 'Amanogawa'

BED D
Hyssopus officinalis
Hyssopus officinalis roseus
Rosmarinus officinalis

BED E
Hypericum perforatum
Levisticum officinale
Satureja montana

BED F
Angelica archangelica
Artemisia abrotanum
Satureja montana

1. *Fagus sylvatica*
2. *Foeniculum vulgare*
3. *Thymus vulgaris*
4. *Melissa officinalis*
5. *Calendula officinalis*
6. *Cynara cardunculus*
7. *Myrrhis odorata*
8. *Artemisia dracunculus*
9. *Allium tuberosum*
10. *Santolina pinnata* ssp.
  neapolitana
11. *Mentha spicata*
12. *Laurus nobilis*
13. *Ruta graveolens*
14. *Origanum vulgare* 'Aureum'
15. *Allium schoenoprasum*

16. *Santolina chamaecyparissus*
  'Lemon Queen'
17. *Artemisia absinthum*
18. *Borago officinalis*
19. *Salix caprea* 'Kilmarnock'
20. *Artemisia* 'Powis Castle'

21. *Malva sylvestris*
22. *Salvia officinalis* 'Icterina'
23. *Pimpinella anisum*
24. Annuals in rotation include:
  Calendula officinalis
  Ocimum basilicum

A Traditional Herb Garden

The lovely house at Old Place Farm, High Halden, Kent, is of medieval origin, dating from the late fifteenth century, so a traditional herb garden design is entirely appropriate in this setting. Ann Eker made her formal ornamental herb garden completely from scratch on the site of what was previously a paddock. The herb garden is a secret garden within a larger one,

and is concealed behind tall hedges. It is enclosed on three sides – on the two long sides by hedges, and on the short, south-facing side by an ancient barn, which is now converted to guest accommodation.

The view from the bench against the barn wall is to the south, facing down the longest vista, and extends into an enclosed lawn, surrounded by

clipped hedges and mature trees, containing a formal allée of *Malus* 'Golden Hornet'. It terminates with a stone sundial on a large plinth. The sense of looking out from an enclosed area into this elegant formal green space prevents any feeling of claustrophobia, so the visitor has the best of both worlds – a feeling of intimate enclosure coupled with a

LEFT: *Pot marigolds as summer bedding in the box parterres, with golden marjoram and curry plant.*
ABOVE: *Camphor, angelica, marjoram and hyssop make an interesting combination in one of the permanent herb beds.*
OPPOSITE: *Marigolds seem to glow in the evening sun, illuminating the herb garden.*

restful long view. At the hot, south-facing end of the garden, large terracotta pots containing tender perennial herbs, mainly scented pelargoniums, are grouped near the seat. Perfumed roses cover the wall of the barn. Enclosed on three sides, this area holds and concentrates the perfume of the fragrant plants.

The herb garden is close to the house, with access to all planting via hard paths, a practical consideration for wet weather. The paths are a lovely combination of reclaimed bricks and York stone. The York stone paving fol-lows a serpentine route among the parterre beds, which makes the garden look wider by breaking up the long brick path which forms the central axis. Those parts of each herb bed that adjoin the central path are planted with different varieties of thyme, which spill out over the edges of the path.

The rectangular herb beds alternate with box-edged parterres, the planting of which is changed twice a year. In spring the parterres contain tulips and forget-me-nots; in summer pot marigolds. The beds containing permanent herb plantings are divided

This sheltered seat catches the sun and has a view out over the herb garden.

into sections by unobtrusive brick edging, which is virtually invisible when the plants are in full leaf but is sufficient to prevent the encroachment of neighbouring plants.

The herbs were chosen for both their decorative and their culinary qualities and, in the way of all good gardeners, Ann Eker has moved or replaced plants that failed to thrive in their original sites, in a process of continual adjustment and growth.

KEY PLANTS

1. *Calendula officinalis*
2. *Buxus sempervirens* 'Suffruticosa'
3. *Thymus × citriodorus* 'Bertram Anderson'
4. *Tanacetum parthenium* 'Aureum'
5. *Hyssopus officinalis*
6. *Tanacetum balsamita* var. *tomentosum*
7. *Levisticum officinale*
8. *Origanum onites*
9. *Angelica archangelica*
10. *Mentha spicata*
11. *Satureja montana*
12. *Tanacetum vulgare*
13. *Lavandula angustifolia*
14. *Thymus × citriodorus* 'Silver Queen'
15. *Mentha × gracilis* 'Variegata'

16. *Monarda didyma*
17. *Anethum graveolens*
18. *Thymus serpyllum*
19. *Salvia officinalis* 'Icterina'
20. *Foeniculum vulgare*
21. *Sanguisorba minor*
22. *Artemisia dracunculus*
23. *Melissa officinalis* 'All Gold'
24. *Agrimonia eupatoria*
25. *Persicaria bistorta*
26. *Salvia officinalis* Purpurascens Group
27. *Thymus × citriodorus* 'Bertram Anderson'
28. *Valeriana officinalis*
29. *Allium schoenoprasum*
30. *Origanum vulgare* 'Aureum'
31. *Mentha suaveolens*
32. *Thymus vulgaris*

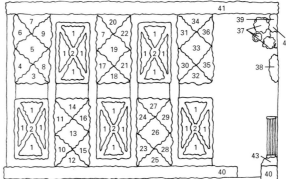

33. *Helichrysum italicum*
34. *Foeniculum vulgare* 'Purpureum'
35. *Matricaria recutita*
36. *Artemisia arborescens*
37. Scented-leaf pelargoniums
38. *Rosa* 'Schoolgirl'

39. *Rosa* 'Cupid'
40. *× Cupressocyparis leylandii* hedge
41. *Taxus baccata*
42. *Vitis vinifera* 'Brant'
43. *Rosmarinus officinalis* 'Benenden Blue'

A Decorative Kitchen Garden

Gunilla and Tim Pickard's garden at Fanners Green in Essex is only one eighth of a hectare (one third of an acre) in size, and the kitchen garden is only part of this. Divided into garden rooms, the area seems much larger than it is. The herb garden layout is in some respects similar to that of Old Place Farm (see pages 64–7), although the planting is less formal.

This garden is a lovely example of abundant informal planting within a formal framework. Both herbs and vegetables are grown here, and the garden has a beguiling cottagey feel, in keeping with the simple weatherboard house. To one side of the central path there are small beds of vegetables; the other side has raised beds constructed from old railway sleepers, containing herbs. The vegetables do well at ground level but the herbs enjoy their slightly elevated position, with the added drainage it provides.

This garden bears its owners' stamp more than most. The paths, mostly of weathered concrete slabs laid directly on the soil surface, are lifted out of the ordinary by Gunilla's own decorative terracotta work at their junctions: each pattern is unique. Gunilla has also made many of her own plant pots; the unusual trellis fashioned from coppiced hazel wands, tied together with pliable willow and decorated with acorns, and

ABOVE: *A simple white seat overlooks the productive kitchen garden.*
RIGHT: Lavandula stoechas *ssp.* pedunculata, *and Alchemilla mollis.*

the charming gate, also of coppiced wood, leading on to the field. The turned wooden finials that decorate the cold frame were made by her son.

Herbs are grouped for decorative effect, and many are used regularly in cooking. A certain amount of self-seeding is permitted, and softens any harsh edges. Gunilla grows some plants for their associations, such as a juniper, which came as a seedling from her parents' summer house in the Swedish countryside (its branches are also used to fuel the barbecue or add flavour to smoked fish). Another juniper, which is in the bed nearest the greenhouse, is there by fortuitous accident. This was heeled in when still a small rooted cutting waiting for a permanent home, but stayed put after Gunilla realized its potential as a windbreak – it is directly in front of the gate leading out on to open farmland.

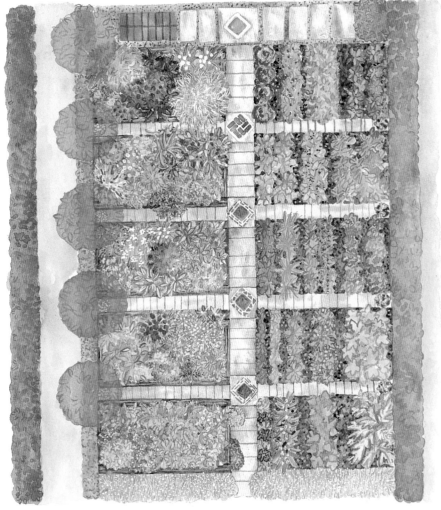

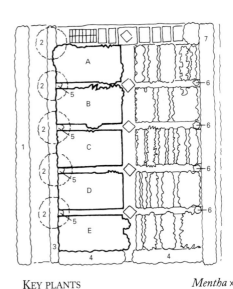

KEY PLANTS
BED A
Allium fistulosum
Atriplex hortensis var. *rubra*
Borago officinalis
Foeniculum vulgare 'Purpureum'
Helichrysum italicum
Juniperus communis f. *suecica*
Rosa gallica var. *officinalis*
BED B
Allium cepa Proliferum Group
Artemisia dracunculus
Buxus sempervirens
Foeniculum vulgare
Lavandula angustifolia

Mentha x *villosa alopecuroides*
Origanum vulgare 'Aureum Crispum'
Rumex acetosa
Salvia lavandulifolia
Tanacetum balsamita var. *tomentosum*
Teucrium chamaedrys 'Nanum'
BED C
Allium schoenoprasum (white)
Levisticum officinale
Myrrhis odorata
Origanum vulgare
Origanum vulgare 'Gold Tip'
Salvia officinalis Purpurascens

Symphytum grandiflorum
Valeriana phu 'Aurea'
BED D
Lavandula stoechas
Mentha x *gracilis*
Rosmarinus officinalis 'Aureus'
Rumex sanguineus
Ruta graveolens
Salvia officinalis 'Icterina'
Santolina pinnata ssp. *neapolitana*
Saponaria officinalis
BED E
Humulus lupulus 'Aureus'
Fragaria vesca 'Multiplex'
Alchemilla mollis

Anthriscus cerefolium
Melissa officinalis
Melissa officinalis 'Aurea'
Tanacetum vulgare var. *crispum*
Thymus polytrichus ssp. *britannicus*

1. *Ligustrum ovalifolium*
2. *Carpinus betulus*
3. *Buxus sempervirens*
4. *Santolina pinnata* ssp. *neapolitana*
5. *Buxus sempervirens* 'Aureovariegata'
6. *Fragaria vesca* 'Multiplex'
7   *Fagus sylvatica* hedge

A Museum Herb Garden

The Geffrye Museum of English domestic interiors at Shoreditch in the East End of London may seem an unlikely home for this delightful walled herb garden. The museum, which is located in what were originally almshouses, comprises a series of historical room sets dating from around 1600 to the 1950s. When funds became available in the early 1990s it was felt that a herb garden would complement the museum very well, since herbs traditionally played such a large part in domestic life. The idea seemed especially apt since Shoreditch had a long history of horticultural activity, although by the early twentieth century the pressures of urban development had squeezed out the once predominant nurseries and market gardens from the area.

The garden was designed to be both beautiful and, given the museum's educational role, informative, hence the grouping of plants according to usage. It is not a historical reproduction: there had never been a herb garden on the site, and the design is strictly contemporary, although its atmosphere is both classical and timeless.

In 1991 the site was completely derelict and piled high with rubbish, but it possessed certain assets: it was both level and square, with some beautiful high eighteenth-century brick walls. Its transformation into the enchanting little garden you see today is largely the result of one woman's vision and commitment. With no previous horticultural training, Christine Lalumia, the museum's deputy director, immersed herself in research – herbal, historical and horticultural – for almost a year, by the end of which the design for the garden was agreed: a simple modern interpretation of a medieval monastic 'paradise garden'. These gardens were usually enclosed and square, divided into quarters by paths, with a well head or fountain at the centre, representing the fount of life.

Plans were drawn up, experts in various fields were consulted, and the site was cleared. A new wall was built

LEFT: Artemisia ludoviciana, Rosa gallica *var.* officinalis *and* Borago officinalis *combine well together in the aromatic beds.*

OPPOSITE: *The elegant seats and trellis arbours were specially designed for the museum. The sound of water spilling over the rim of the fountain is just loud enough to distract attention from the noise of passing traffic, without being intrusive. A fig tree* (Ficus carica) *strikes an exotic note among the climbing roses which cover the wall, and the use of* Lavandula angustifolia *'Hidcote' along the central borders of the aromatic beds draws the planting design together.*

to complete the square on the east side of the garden, using reclaimed brick carefully chosen to match the existing old brickwork. The paths are also made of reclaimed brick, and the arbour plinths are built of eighteenth-century York stone, a material used extensively elsewhere in the museum grounds. The choice of old landscaping materials has contributed greatly to the garden's atmosphere of maturity.

The fine fountain at the centre of the Geffrye garden is a recent addition. Specially commissioned, and designed by local artist Kate Malone, its musical bubbling masks the noise of nearby traffic and makes an irresistible focal point for the garden. Seating plays an important role in attracting visitors into the herb garden and encouraging them to stay and to observe. There are three lovely romantic trellis arbours, covered with roses and other perfumed climbing plants, which provide a welcome refuge from the bustle of inner city life.

Although it is public, the Geffrye herb garden has not the faintest whiff of the municipal about it. Every aspect

The spiky leaves of orris (Iris pallida) *and the spires of the foxgloves provide good contrast of form among the softer outlines of the other aromatic herbs.*

of the garden has been painstakingly considered, with the result that its atmosphere is more that of a favourite private retreat which we the public are privileged to enter. It is obviously very well loved and used, both by locals and museum visitors.

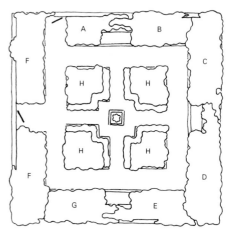

KEY PLANTS
BED A: BEE PLANTS
Verbascum thapsus
Galium odoratum
Marrubium vulgare
Agastache foeniculum
BED B: DYE PLANTS
Isatis tinctoria
Reseda luteola
Genista tinctoria
Rubia tinctorum

BED C: SEASONING HERBS
Levisticum officinale
Angelica archangelica
Allium fistulosum
Salvia officinalis
BED D: SALAD HERBS
Rumex acetosa
Sanguisorba minor
Atriplex hortensis var. *rubra*
Thymus x *citriodorus*
 'Fragrantissimus'

BED E: COSMETIC HERBS
Phytolacca americana
Achillea millefolium
Salvia sclarea
Sempervivum tectorum
BED F: MEDICINAL HERBS
Pulmonaria officinalis
Symphytum officinale
Digitalis purpurea
Sambucus nigra
Stachys officinalis

Oenothera biennis
BED G: HOUSEHOLD HERBS
Saponaria officinalis
Tanacetum balsamita
Alchemilla mollis
Artemisia vulgaris
BED H: AROMATIC HERBS
Rosmarinus officinalis
Monarda didyma
Iris pallida
Mentha species

A Herb Parterre

This herb garden is part of a much larger garden covering several acres, attached to the Ballymaloe cookery school at Kinoith in County Cork, Ireland. As well as being decorative, it is very much a working garden, designed to supply the kitchens of the cookery school. Huge by most standards – one eighth of a hectare (one third of an acre) – this relatively new garden was inspired by the famous gardens of Villandry in France. The impressive beech hedges on either side of the herb garden are thought to have been planted around the middle of the last century, but by the time Darina and Tim Allen began the garden restoration in the early 1980s, they had become badly overgrown. They needed hard pruning – always a nerve-wracking operation since beech does not always regrow successfully from old wood. Luckily the risk paid off and the hedges have now been restored to their former glory.

The precise geometry of the parterre beds, edged in low clipped box, lends structure even in the depths of winter,

BELOW: *Cardoons add a sculptural element to the exuberant planting.*
OPPOSITE: *Maximum informality of planting combines with maximum formality of structure in this garden.*

when many herbs are dormant and below ground. For height during the summer months, scarlet runner beans, originally introduced into Northern Europe for their ornamental value, are trained on decorative metal obelisks in the smaller circular beds in the centre of the garden.

The beds of the parterre are laid out in a symmetrical living carpet, a style of gardening which cries out to be viewed from above. The Allens have obliged, by installing a tree-house viewing platform in one of the mature trees to the south of the herb garden, a device not without historical precedent.

In a garden such as this, which relies on large-scale planting and clipped symmetry for effect, the hard landscaping needs to be both uniform throughout and unobtrusive, so the pale gravel paths used here are an excellent choice, throwing the dense green of the box into stark relief. The planting layout is in itself so ornamental that it requires little by way of artificial adornment. The garden has a sundial, a traditional herb garden ornament, and a fine, but not too elaborate, metal seat with a south-facing view down the long central axis.

The best way of keeping any herb garden looking reasonably tidy is to harvest the herbs frequently, and with the demands placed on the garden by the cookery school this tends to happen as a matter of course. To preserve the full impact of the design the hedges

ABOVE LEFT: *Although this is a large herb garden, the scale of paths, gates and entrances makes it feel quite intimate.*
ABOVE RIGHT: *In the smaller circular beds, decorative metal obelisks (which in summer are covered with runner beans) as well as taller herbs such as angelica add height and interest, drawing the eye to different sections of the garden.*

must be well maintained, but this style of herb gardening can actually be quite forgiving with regard to planting detail. Particularly where a large range of herbs are grown, as here, the formal structure gives a coherence to the design that is difficult to achieve by any other means.

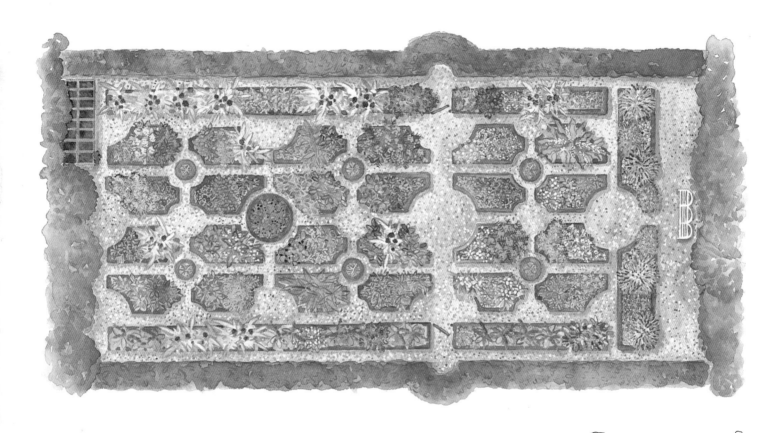

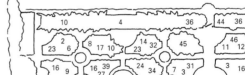

KEY PLANTS

1. *Fragaria vesca*
2. *Angelica archangelica*
3. *Origanum onites*
4. *Mentha suaveolens*
5. *Ocimum basilicum*
6. *Laurus nobilis*
7. *Borago officinalis*
8. *Mentha* x *villosa alopecuroides*
9. *Foeniculum vulgare* 'Purpureum'
10. *Cynara cardunculus*
11. *Matricaria recutita*
12. *Anthriscus cerefolium*
13. *Allium schoenoprasum*
14. *Symphytum officinale*
15. *Coriandrum sativum*
16. *Petroselinum crispum*
17. *Anethum graveolens*
18. *Foeniculum vulgare*
19. *Digitalis purpurea*

20. *Artemisia dracunculus*
21. *Allium tuberosum*
22. *Mentha* x *gracilis*
23. *Origanum vulgare* 'Aureum'
24. *Salvia officinalis* 'Icterina'
25. *Armoracia rusticana*
26. *Lavandula angustifolia*
27. *Melissa officinalis*
28. *Levisticum officinale*
29. *Myrtus communis*
30. *Tropaeolum majus*
31. *Origanum vulgare*
32. *Mentha* x *piperita*
33. *Calendula officinalis*
34. *Salvia officinalis* Purpurascens Group
35. *Eruca vesicaria* ssp. *sativa*
36. *Rosa* 'Zéphirine Drouhin'
37. *Rosmarinus officinalis*
38. *Salvia officinalis*
39. *Sanguisorba minor*

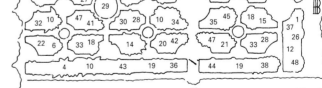

40. *Thymus vulgaris* 'Silver Posie'
41. *Rumex acetosa*
42. *Mentha spicata*
43. *Hesperis matronalis*
44. Scented-leaf pelargoniums
45. *Tanacetum vulgare*

46. *Thymus vulgaris*
47. *Melissa officinalis* 'Aurea'
48. *Thymus* 'Doone Valley'
49. *Fagus sylvatica* hedge

Buxus hedges round all beds

A Cottage Herb Garden

Christina Stapley's garden, at Brook Cottages, East Meon, Hampshire, is devoted entirely to herbs. It covers one eighth of a hectare (one third of an acre), and is divided into themed areas. Although this garden is similar in size to that at Ballymaloe cookery school (see pages 74–7), the divisions make it seem much smaller, in scale with the seventeenth-century thatched cottage to which it is attached.

Breaking up the site in this way has practical advantages when a large area is to be cultivated by just one or two people, particularly on a limited budget as was the case here. One area at a time can be completed, giving the gardener a steady sense of progress and spreading the cost and effort.

Throughout the garden the planting is mainly according to use, although within these constraints

Christina goes to a lot of trouble to ensure that adjacent plants are compatible, both aesthetically and in terms of the conditions they enjoy.

A public footpath runs along the west boundary, and many people must surely make detours along it in order to see this lovely garden. Christina has considered the view from this path when planning her planting schemes, from a child's as well as an adult's

perspective, and has made an enticing, welcoming garden, not one that seeks to exclude. The scale of the garden is quite small – the seats, covered way, paths, even the trellis mesh, are smaller than they might appear from the photographs. This gives it a particular charm, as all the diminutive features are in perfect proportion with each other; it has an almost fairy-tale quality, which is accentuated by the old-fashioned beauty of the timber-framed thatched cottage.

Inspired by her fascination with Elizabethan knot gardens, Christina began by creating a knot for culinary and physic herbs, using some typical features of the period. There is a tiny camomile seat which is watched over by a pair of hand-carved wooden birds made by D.J. Smith, and sheltered by a trellis arbour clad in perfumed climbing plants. The open knot is bordered on one side by a trellis covered way into which 'windows' have been cut, permitting one to view the garden from within. The covered way also makes a cool oasis of shade on a hot summer's day, in which to sit and rest.

OPPOSITE AND RIGHT: *The idea for the covered way adjoining the culinary and physic knot gardens at Brook Cottages dates from the Elizabethan era, when ladies were supposed to retain a pale complexion. Clad in roses and other perfumed plants, in summer it becomes a scented, shady corridor.*

The medical astrology beds were inspired by the work of the seventeenth-century herbalist, Nicholas Culpeper. He considered the astrological signs of medicinal herbs to be of great importance, and so these beds are grouped by their signs of the zodiac.

The area currently used as seed-beds is now earmarked for a children's corner, since there are so many young visitors to the garden. Christina is planning a living tunnel with a secret hiding place, a nut tree, another camomile seat, a bird table and a basket sculpture, among other things.

The garden has a mount, a feature popular in Elizabethan times, which in winter affords a view down on to the Serenity knot garden, which is composed of herbs thought to possess soothing and calming properties. In summer the view is obscured by luxuriant plant growth.

The mount is planted with herbs for homeopathy and essential oils, mainly so that visitors can see the plants from which these remedies are made. They are not grown in sufficient quantity to extract oil or make homeopathic remedies; it would be impractical to do so, since immense volumes would be needed, but Christina is a teacher at heart, and something of a herb missionary.

Like most people who grow herbs to use in cooking or medicine, Christina prefers to garden organically.

Besides making her own garden compost and growing herbs to be used for fertilizer and insecticide, she also grows many varieties of herbs which attract bees and other beneficial wildlife into the garden.

TOP: *Apothecary's roses, golden hops, fennel and York and Lancaster roses growing on the covered way.*
ABOVE: *Sea holly, rue and golden marjoram make a wonderful combination of forms and colours.*

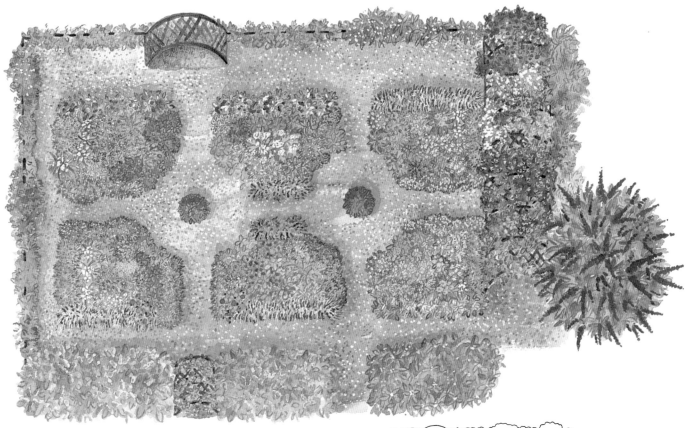

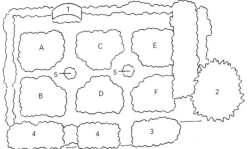

KEY PLANTS
CULINARY BEDS
BED A
Allium sativum
Allium schoenoprasum
Anthriscus cerefolium
Levisticum officinale
Melissa officinalis
Myrrhis odorata
Origanum vulgare
Rosmarinus officinalis
BED B
Artemisia dracunculus
Coriandrum sativum
Foeniculum vulgare
Lavandula angustifolia
Ocimum basilicum
Origanum vulgare
Petroselinum crispum
Sanguisorba minor
Satureja montana
Tropaeolum majus

BED C
Angelica archangelica
Mentha suaveolens 'Variegata'
Mentha x *gracilis*
Mentha x *piperita*
Primula vulgaris
Salvia officinalis
BED D
Borago officinalis
Calendula officinalis
Carum carvi
Hyssopus officinalis
Thymus x *citriodorus*

PHYSIC BEDS
BED E
Achillea millefolium
Chamaemelum nobile
Melissa officinalis
Rosmarinus officinalis
Tanacetum parthenium
Valeriana officinalis

BED F
Althaea officinalis
Anethum graveolens
Hypericum perforatum
Inula helenium
Leonorus cardiaca
Marrubium vulgare
Oenothera biennis
Salvia officinalis Purpurascens
  Group

CLIMBERS ON COVERED WAY
Humulus lupulus 'Aureus'
Lonicera japonica 'Aureoreticulata'
Lonicera periclymenum 'Belgica'
Rosa banksiae var. *banksiae*
Rosa x *damascena versicolor*

1. Camomile seat
2. *Buddleja davidii*
3. *Cornus alba* 'Sibirica'
4. *Syringa vulgaris*
5. *Laurus nobilis*

A Country Herb Garden

This small herb garden within a garden makes excellent use of limited space, without being claustrophobic. Like the Geffrye Museum garden (see pages 70–3), it is inspired by the monastic paradise gardens of the medieval period.

Randall Anderson, its designer, employs various devices to create a smooth integration into the setting. The back wall of the conservatory is densely clothed with foliage: when viewed from a distance it gives the impression of another garden waiting to be explored. The wide coping round the pool is made from the same type of reconstituted Cotswold stone used in the paving, avoiding any jarring visual break. The pool edge is almost an extension of the path, and the eye is led in one sweep along the main axis of the garden. The coping around the pool slopes slightly, so the water level can be raised, submerging most of the edge, and increasing the surface area. The fountain can be set to produce ripples, a bubble or a taller jet to give the garden quite a different feel.

The uncluttered design combines formality of outline with informality of planting in the best gardening tradition.

BELOW: *The pleasing symmetry of this herb garden is seen here to good effect.*
OPPOSITE: *The abundant planting, with some herbs allowed to self-seed, softens the formality of the design.*

The garden is introspective in aspect, the pool acting as a strong central focus, while the smaller L-shaped beds nestle within the larger ones, echoing their shape, directing the attention inwards and smoothing the visual transition from boundary to centre.

All the beds in this garden are raised, although the planting is so full that this is apparent only during the garden's dormant period. The earth is held back by wooden boards about 15cm (6in) high, which serve a twofold purpose – they emphasize the bold geometric lines of the garden in winter, and the raised soil level also improves drainage, aiding the survival of plants which might otherwise succumb to winter cold and wet.

The hard landscaping is not allowed to dominate but acts as a foil for the softly billowing plant shapes. The balance between hard and soft is handled with great sensitivity.

A conservatory was added at the time the herb garden was made, to close the gap between existing garden

ABOVE: *Pot-grown topiary lends instant height and structure to the herb garden.*

buildings and create a focal point at one end of the main axis. The central positioning of the door is important, leading the eye smoothly onwards and tempting the visitor to enter.

The garden is planted with a profusion of aromatic, culinary and medicinal herbs. Plants are squeezed into every corner – not a patch of bare

earth is visible, and there is a sense that at any moment the whole thing might run out of control, which makes this planting very exciting. Standard hollies give shape and coherence to the looser herb plantings, providing structure, height and winter interest. The garden is designed to be at its best from late spring to midsummer. In late summer, when the planting has lost its freshness, many plants are cut back hard to stimulate new growth, which revitalizes the garden and keeps it looking good into autumn.

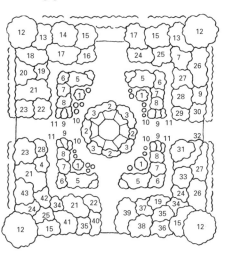

KEY PLANTS
1. *Ilex* × *altaclerensis* 'Golden King'
2. *Santolina chamaecyparissus*
3. *Lavandula* 'Rosea'
4. *Allium tuberosum*
5. *Artemisia pontica*
6. *Helichrysum angustifolium*
7. *Origanum onites*
8. *Hyssopus officinalis*
9. *Allium schoenoprasum*
10. *Fragaria alpina*
11. *Thymus* × *citriodorus*

12. *Morus nigra*
13. *Smyrnium olusatrum*
14. *Foeniculum vulgare* 'Purpureum'
15. *Angelica archangelica*
16. Pots of *Lippia citriodora* and scented-leaf pelargoniums
17. *Saponaria officinalis*
18. *Salvia sclarea* var. *turkestanica*
19. *Allium cepa* Proliferum Group
20. *Mentha* × *smithiana*
21. *Ruta graveolens* 'Variegata'

22. *Lavandula* 'Twickel Purple'
23. *Salvia officinalis*
24. *Salvia officinalis* Purpurascens Group
25. *Mentha rotundifolia*
26. *Dipsacus fullonum*
27. *Mentha rotundifolia variegata*
28. *Lavandula officinalis*
29. *Dianthus caesius*
30. *Iris* 'Jane Phillips'
31. *Lavandula lanata*
32. *Dianthus* hybrids

33. *Rosmarinus* 'Miss Jessopp's Upright'
34. *Petroselinum crispum*
35. *Monarda didyma* hybrids
36. *Anchusa azurea*
37. *Mentha spicata*
38. *Ruta graveolens* 'Jackman's Blue'
39. *Salvia argentea*
40. *Melissa officinalis*
41. *Tanacetum vulgare*
42. *Rumex acetosa*
43. *Borago officinalis*

FIFTY DECORATIVE HERBS

This guide does not purport to be a medical herbal. While many herbs are perfectly safe to eat and touch, this does not apply across the board. Some herbs are extremely powerful in their effects, and all should be treated with respect. Before using a herb in any way, make sure that you are well informed about its properties and potential hazards. Herbs may be 'natural' but 'natural' is not the same as 'safe' – some of the plants described here, benificent and healing if used correctly, can be fatal if misused. This is not a reason to avoid them. Why forgo the pleasure of their beauty when a little prudence is all that is required?

Children should be taught from an early age not to touch, pick or eat any part of a plant, unless they are certain of its identity and know it to be safe. Some perfectly benign plants have deadly relatives of very similar appearance, and even 'safe' plants may recently have been sprayed with a toxic chemical.

RECOMMENDED VARIETIES are given in addition to, not instead of, the species named in the main heading. The species described are all attractive garden plants in their own right. Where two or more symbols are given for light requirements, the one occurring first in the line is to be preferred, the second tolerated; thus ☀ and ☀ is interpreted as 'does best in full sun but tolerates partial shade'.

KEY TO SYMBOLS
☀ Requires full sun
☀ Requires partial shade
☀ Requires shade
🐝 Good bee plant
✚ Medicinal use
🌷 Cosmetic use
🍴 Culinary use
⚱ Used for teas/tisanes
⚜ Dye plant
⚓ Unsuitable for container growing
☠ Warning – hazardous

Agastache foeniculum **anise hyssop**
Height: 60cm (2ft) Spread: 30cm (1ft) ☀ 🐝 🍴
Slightly tender perennial, with upright habit, for fertile, moisture-retentive soil. Mid-green foliage plant with purple flowers. Whole plant is aromatic. Season of interest: summer. Propagate by sowing seed under glass in early spring, taking softwood cuttings in spring or semi-ripe cuttings in summer. Take cuttings in case of winter losses. In winter, protect mature plants from extremes of cold; young plants should be kept dry and frost-free.

Ajuga reptans **bugle**
H: 12–30cm (5–12in) S: indefinite ☀ ☀ 🐝 ✚
Hardy perennial for moisture-retentive soil. Various leaf colours are available, but most have blue flowers. Season of interest: late spring, early summer, but leaves good all year. Propagate by division from early spring to mid-autumn. Good weed-suppressing groundcover. Needs digging up periodically and replanting with some of the more vigorous new offsets. Prone to slug damage on occasions.
RECOMMENDED VARIETIES: *Ajuga reptans* 'Catlins Giant' – larger form, vigorous with glossy bronze leaves; *A. reptans* 'Atropurpurea' – medium-sized, bronze leaves; *A. reptans* 'Tricolor' – grey-green, pink and cream variegated leaves.

Alchemilla mollis **lady's mantle**
H: 20cm (8in) S: 45cm (18in) ☀ ☀ ✚
Hardy perennial for any except boggy soil. Soft green foliage plant with greeny yellow flowers. Season of interest: spring to autumn. Propagate by seed or division in spring or autumn for both methods. Sometimes a prolific self-seeder. When plant looks jaded in late summer, trim back and it will soon regenerate.
RECOMMENDED VARIETIES: *Alchemilla conjuncta* and *A. alpina* are both pretty and less prolific seeders, needing drier conditions than *A. mollis*.

Allium cepa Proliferum Group **tree onion**
H: to 1.5m (5ft) S: 30cm (1ft) ☀ 🍴
Hardy perennial with upright habit for fertile, free-draining soil. Blue-green, glaucous foliage plant with insignificant white flowers. Whole plant is aromatic. Season of interest: spring and summer. To propagate, plant out bulbils which form among the flower heads in summer.

Grow in a sheltered spot (not tender, but may blow over) and keep well watered throughout growing season.

Allium schoenoprasum chives

H: 30cm (1ft) S: 15cm (6in) ☀ ☼ ▮●▮ ⊞
Hardy perennial with upright habit for any reasonably moist soil. Mid-green leaves with light mauve, pink or white flowers. Leaves and flowers are aromatic. Season of interest: spring to autumn. Sow seed outdoors in spring. Divide clumps in early spring. Mulch with well-rotted compost in autumn. Make sure soil does not dry out, as this makes leaf tips go brown. After flowering, cut back to 12cm (5in) to promote another flush of growth. Pot up and bring in for a winter supply.
RECOMMENDED VARIETIES: *Allium schoenoprasum roseum* is a pink flowered form; The white form of *A. schoenoprasum* has white flowers; *A. schoenoprasum* var. *sibiricum* is grows to 30–45cm (12–18in).

Anethum graveolens dill

H: 1m (3ft 3in) S: 25cm (10in) ☀ ▮●▮ ⊞
Half-hardy annual for free-draining soil. Good mid-green foliage plant with yellow

LEFT: Agastache foeniculum
ABOVE: Anethum graveolens *'Mammoth'*

flowers and aromatic leaves forming upright feathery plumes. Season of interest: summer. Propagate by seed from early spring to early summer. Dislikes disturbance, so sow seed in modules or in situ. Keep well away from fennel, as they interbreed. May need staking.

Angelica archangelica angelica

H: 1.8m (6ft) S: 1m (3ft 3in) ☀ ☼ ▮●▮ ⊞ ☠
Hardy biennial or short-lived perennial for fertile, moisture-retentive soil. Mid-green foliage plant with green or cream flowers. Whole plant is aromatic. Season of interest: late spring to midsummer. Propagate by fresh seed in autumn. When it has set seed it will die, but it can be maintained as a perennial for 3–4 years by removing the flower heads before seed is produced. It self-seeds prolifically, so remove seed-heads before they are ripe to avoid this. Needs plenty of moisture, so add organic material to the soil in generous amounts. Prone to blackfly – spray with horticultural soap.

RECOMMENDED VARIETIES: *Angelica gigas* – lovely species with dark purple flowers.
✳ Can be toxic if taken in very large quantities. Occasional culinary use is OK, but for medicinal use, consult a qualified practitioner. May cause blistering in some people if handled in strong sunlight.

Anthemis tinctoria dyer's camomile

H: 1m (3ft 3in) S: 1m (3ft 3in) ☀ ▼ ☠
Hardy perennial for free-draining soil. Mid-green leaves with soft yellow flowers. Season of interest: summer. Propagate by division or softwood cuttings in spring. Prune quite hard after flowering to encourage a good leafy rosette for over-wintering. Winter treatment: prevent waterlogging.
RECOMMENDED VARIETIES: *Anthemis tinctoria* 'E.C. Buxton' – very floriferous, with lemon flowers.
✳ Dye plant only – not to be taken.

Artemisia abrotanum southernwood

H: 1m (3ft 3in S: 1m (3ft 3in) ☀ ⊞ ☙ ☡
Hardy evergreen shrub for free-draining soil. Grey-green foliage plant with insignificant flowers and aromatic leaves. Season of interest: spring to autumn. Propagate by softwood or semi-ripe cuttings in spring and summer respectively. Upright habit, although can be clipped into a tight but feathery mound in the growing season when there is no danger of frost. Stands hard pruning in warm weather. Site it where you can pick an aromatic leaf in passing. Winter treatment – prevent waterlogging.
✳ Not to be taken during pregnancy.

Atriplex hortensis orach, red orach, mountain spinach

H: to 1.2m (4ft) S: 30cm (1ft) ☀ ☼ ▮●▮
Hardy annual for fertile, free-draining soil. Excellent green or bronze foliage plant with insignificant flowers. Season of

interest: spring to autumn. Propagate by seed in spring. A prolific self-seeder – remove flower heads to avoid this if desired. If a small, bushy plant is needed, keep pinching out growing points.
RECOMMENDED VARIETIES: *Atriplex hortensis* var. *rubra*.

Borago officinalis **borage**

H: 60cm (2ft) S: 45cm (18in) ☼ ✻ ✚ ¶◖ ☠
Hardy annual for free-draining soil. Good, soft green, hairy foliage plant with blue flowers. Season of interest: summer. Propagate by seed in spring. Dead-head regularly to prolong flowering. Self-seeds profusely so remove seed pods.
✱ May cause an allergic reaction

Buxus sempervirens **box**

H: to 5m (15ft) S: to 5m (15ft) ☼ ✻ ✚ ☠
Hardy evergreen shrub for any soil. Season of interest: year-round. Propagate dwarf box by division in spring, and ordinary box by semi-ripe cuttings in summer. Feed well and prune quite hard in spring to encourage dense new growth. Protect from extremes of cold and wet, especially when plants are young.
RECOMMENDED VARIETIES: *Buxus sempervirens* 'Suffruticosa' is the dwarf box often used for knot garden hedging; *B. sempervirens* 'Elegantissima' is a good variegated form.
✱ Use only under qualified medical supervision. All parts of the plant are toxic if eaten and it can also irritate skin.

Calendula officinalis **marigold**

H: to 60cm (2ft) S: to 60cm (2ft) ☼ ✚ ¶◖
Hardy annual for any soil type except boggy. Mid-green leaves with orange or yellow flowers. Season of interest: summer to autumn. Propagate by seed in spring or autumn. Regular dead-heading prolongs flowering. Slugs and snails like the young leaves, and later on

Atriplex hortensis *var.* rubra *(seedlings)*

blackfly can be a problem – treat with horticultural soap. Protect seedlings from extremes of wet and cold.

Chamaemelum nobile **camomile, Roman or lawn**

H: 10cm (4in) S: indefinite ☼ ✚ ❧
Hardy perennial for free-draining, fertile soil. Bright green foliage plant with white and yellow flowers. All parts of plant are scented when crushed. Season of interest: all year. Propagate by division or softwood cuttings from spring to autumn. Weed regularly as camomile lawns are not dense enough to suppress all weeds. Water in times of drought, and trim to maintain density of cover. Remove offsets in spring and use to fill any gaps. Protect from extremes of wet and cold.
RECOMMENDED VARIETIES: *Chamaemelum nobile* 'Treneague', the non-flowering clone, is recommended for lawns and seats; *C. nobile* 'Flore Pleno' has pretty, small double white flowers.
✱ Do not use the essential oil during pregnancy.

Convallaria majalis **lily-of-the-valley**

H: 20cm (8in) S: indefinite ☼ ✚ ☠
Hardy perennial for fertile, moisture-retentive soil. Soft green foliage plant with white, scented flowers. Season of interest: late spring to early summer. Propagate by division in early autumn. Can be invasive; site where it can spread. Pot rhizomes in autumn for forcing in a cool greenhouse.
RECOMMENDED VARIETIES: *Convallaria majalis* 'Vic Pawlowski's Gold' has stunning yellow-striped leaves, but is very rare and slow to increase.
✱ Use only under qualified medical supervision. Poisonous if eaten.

Crocus sativus **saffron**

H: 15cm (6in) S: 8cm (3in) ☼ ¶◖
Slightly tender bulb for free-draining, fertile soil. Green leaves with purple flowers. Season of interest: autumn. Propagate by sowing seed or dividing the clumps of corms in early autumn. Plant corms at least 10cm (4in) deep. Winter treatment: prevent waterlogging and protect from extreme cold.

Dianthus **pinks**

H: to 60cm (2ft) S: to 60cm (2ft) ☼
Hardy perennial for free-draining, alkaline soil. Grey or green foliage plant with scented flowers in various colours. Season of interest: summer. Propagate by pulling out new growing tips and using as cuttings in summer. Pinch out growing points to maintain a bushy habit. Short-lived, so take cuttings. Winter treatment: prevent waterlogging. There are many good varieties to choose from.

Digitalis **foxglove**

H: 1.5m (5ft) S: 40cm (16in) ☼ ✻ ✚ ☠
Hardy biennial or perennial for free-draining soil. Mid-green leaves with mauve, pink, white or yellow flowers.

Season of interest: summer. Propagate by seed or softwood cuttings from spring to midsummer. Seeds need light to germinate; propagate selected forms from softwood cuttings. Protect plants from severe cold in their first winter.
RECOMMENDED VARIETIES: *Digitalis purpurea* – mauve flowers; *D. purpurea* f. *albiflora* – white flowers; *D. purpurea* ssp. *heywoodii* – silver-grey, felted leaves and white flowers; *D. lutea* – green leaves and yellow flowers. There are many other species and cultivars – those listed are both attractive and medicinal.
✻ Highly toxic. Use only under qualified medical supervision.

Filipendula ulmaria meadowsweet
H: to 1.2m (4ft) S: 60cm (2ft) ☼ ☀ ✚
Hardy perennial for moisture-retentive, fertile soil. Green, gold or variegated foliage plant with cream flowers and aromatic leaves. Season of interest: summer. Propagate by division in early autumn. Winter treatment: protect young plants.
RECOMMENDED VARIETIES: *Filipendula ulmaria* 'Aurea' – yellow-leaved form; *F. ulmaria* 'Variegata' – green and yellow leaf variegations, which fade over the growing season.

Foeniculum vulgare fennel
H: 1.5m (5ft) S: 45cm (18in) ☼ ✚ ♠ |●| ♈
Hardy perennial for fertile, free-draining soil. Excellent green or bronze foliage plant with yellow flowers and feathery, aromatic leaves. Season of interest: spring to autumn. Propagate by seed in spring. Self-sows readily, but transplant when small, as plants produce a long tap root which dislikes being moved.
RECOMMENDED VARIETIES: *Foeniculum vulgare* 'Purpureum' is the bronze form, but the plain green is also a lovely plant.

Calendula officinalis

Galium odoratum sweet woodruff
H: 15cm (6in) S: indefinite ☼ ☀ ✚ |●|
Hardy perennial with spreading habit for free-draining soil. Bright green foliage plant with white flowers. The entire plant is aromatic, especially when dried. Season of interest: spring to early summer. Propagate by dividing plants in early spring, or sow fresh seed in autumn in a coldframe. Good for dry shade.

Humulus lupulus hop
H: to 6m (20ft) ☼ ☀ ✚ |●| ☠
Hardy perennial climber for free-draining soil. Green or golden foliage plant with green flowers. Season of interest: spring to late autumn. Propagate by leaf bud cuttings in late spring. Very vigorous, so plant where it will not swamp its neighbours. The plants can be male or female – only the latter produce usable hops. Cut to ground level in autumn, mulch, and keep quite dry through winter.
RECOMMENDED VARIETIES: *Humulus lupulus* 'Aureus' – the golden hop.
✻ Can irritate skin.

Hyssopus officinalis hyssop H: 70cm (2ft 3in)
S: 80cm (2ft 9in) ☼ ✸ ✚ |●| ☠
Hardy perennial for free-draining soil. Dark green, aromatic leaves with blue flowers. Season of interest: midsummer to early autumn. Propagate from seed sown under glass in early spring, or take cuttings from late spring to early summer. Prune immediately after flowering, to retain compact growth habit. Winter treatment: prevent waterlogging.
RECOMMENDED VARIETIES: *Hyssopus officinalis* f. *albus* has white flowers; *H. officinalis roseus* is pink.
✻ Can have unpleasant side-effects in some people. Take only under qualified medical supervision.

Iris 'Florentina' orris iris
H: to 1m (3ft 3in) S: indefinite ☼ ♣ ☠ ♈
Hardy perennial for free-draining soil. Grey-green foliage plant with white flowers. Season of interest: summer. Propagate by division in late summer. Rots if wet – allow to bake in hot weather, leave part of rhizome above ground. Winter treatment: prevent waterlogging.
✻ Can cause vomiting and diarrhoea – do not eat it and wash hands after handling.

Laurus nobilis bay
H: to 8m (27ft) S: to 3m (10ft) ☼ ☀ |●|
Slightly tender evergreen tree or shrub for fertile soil. Dark green leaves with insignificant flowers. Season of interest: all year. Propagate by semi-ripe cuttings in late summer. Cuttings are slow to root, needing high humidity, bottom heat and rooting hormone. Bay can be kept within bounds by clipping in spring – makes good topiary. Train standards as described on page 48. Occasional insect pests can be controlled with horticultural soap. Winter treatment: protect plants from extreme cold – especially when young.

Lavandula angustifolia **lavender** H: to 1m
(3ft 3in) S: to 1m (3ft 3in) ☼ 🐝 ✚ ❘●❘
Variably hardy evergreen shrub for free-
draining soil. Grey foliage with violet,
blue, pink or white flowers. Leaves and
flowers are aromatic, but the intensity
varies between types. Season of interest:
summer. Propagate by softwood cuttings
in early summer or seed in autumn for
seed. Prune in spring, but do not cut back
to old (brown) wood. Prune again in late
summer. Prone to occasional attack by
fungal diseases in wet weather. Cut out
and destroy affected areas as soon as
trouble is spotted. Winter treatment:
some species need frost-free conditions,
all need protection from waterlogging.
RECOMMENDED VARIETIES: *Lavandula
angustifolia* – the most hardy; *L.
angustifolia* 'Hidcote' – large with fine,
dark purple flowers; *L. stoechas* and its
cultivars are all lovely with tufted flowers;
L. pinnata and *L. dentata* have excellent
foliage and flowers, but are not hardy.

Levisticum officinale **lovage**
H: to 2m (6½ft) S: to 1m (3ft 3in) ☼ ☼ ✚ ❘●❘
Hardy perennial for moisture-retentive,
free-draining soil. Soft green foliage plant
with greeny yellow flowers. Season of
interest: spring to autumn. Propagate by
seed or division in spring. Plants can be
kept small by regular picking – young
leaves are best for kitchen use anyway.

Lonicera **honeysuckle**
H: to 10m (33ft) ☼ ☼ 🐝 ✚
Hardy perennial climber for fertile, free-
draining soil. Green leaves with yellow,
pink, cream or scarlet, scented flowers.
Season of interest: summer. Propagate by
semi-ripe cuttings in summer or from
hardwood cuttings in autumn. Can be
trained as a standard, or allowed to
scramble over a robust support or arbour.
Prune after flowering, and in spring to

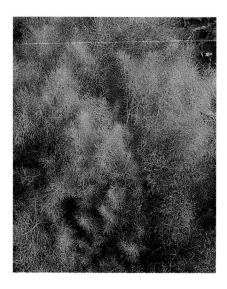

Foeniculum vulgare

keep it within bounds.
RECOMMENDED VARIETIES: *Lonicera* x
americana – highly scented, pink buds
and yellow flowers; *L. periclymenum*
'Serotina' – highly scented, dark purple
flowers, *L. japonica* 'Aureoreticulata' –
creamy flowers and yellow-veined green
leaves. Many other lovely forms exist.

Mentha **mint** H: to 80cm (2ft 9in)
S: indefinite ☼ ☼ ✚ ❘●❘ ☠
Hardy perennial for moisture-retentive,
fertile soil. Green or variegated foliage
plant with purple flowers and aromatic
leaves. Season of interest: spring to
autumn. Propagate by root cuttings or
division any time in the growing season,
trimming top growth to prevent wilting
while roots establish. Most mints spread
rampantly, so are best confined – try
growing them in large pots. Revitalize
plants by frequent propagation from the
new growth at the outside of the clump,
discarding the old centre. Mints can be
prone to rust – cut off the affected parts.
An old gardeners' way of defeating over-

wintering rust spores is to pile dry straw
on the dormant plants and set fire to it.
To prevent hybridizing when growing
several different mints in proximity, cut
off flowers before they open.
RECOMMENDED VARIETIES: *Mentha
suaveolens* 'Variegata' (pineapple mint),
with soft green and cream variegated
leaves; *M. longifolia* (buddleja mint), with
pointed mauve flower spikes; *M.* x *gracilis*
(ginger mint) with yellow-variegated
leaves. *M. requienii* (Corsican mint) is a
slightly tender carpeter only 1cm (½in)
high, with an indefinite spread.
✱ Peppermint oil may cause an allergic
reaction – do not use on babies.

Myrrhis odorata **sweet cicely**
H: 80cm (2ft 9in) S: 60cm (2ft) ☼ ❘●❘ ☠
Hardy perennial for fertile, free-draining
soil. Mid-green foliage plant with white
flowers and aromatic leaves. Season of
interest: spring to late summer. Propagate
from seed sown in autumn in a coldframe
or by division in early spring. Plants will
regrow from fragments of root left in soil,
so try to avoid moving it. Dormant for a
very short period in winter.
✱ Very large quantities might be toxic.

Myrtus communis **myrtle**
H: to 3m (10ft) S: to 3m (10ft) ☼ ✚
Slightly tender evergreen shrub for fertile,
free-draining soil. Glossy dark green
leaves with white flowers. Both leaves and
flowers are scented. Season of interest:
spring to midsummer. Propagate from
cuttings between late spring and late
summer. Best grown against a south-
facing wall in cooler climates. Winter
treatment: cover with fleece in frosty
weather and prevent waterlogging.
RECOMMENDED VARIETIES: *Myrtus
communis* ssp. *tarentina*, to 2m (6½ft);
M. communis 'Variegata' has cream-
variegated leaves, tinged pink in autumn.

Nepeta species and cultivars **catmint**
H: 45–75cm (1½–2½ft) S: 45–75cm (1½–2½ft)
☀ 🐝
Hardy perennial for free-draining soil. Grey-green foliage plant with hazy blue flowers. Leaves and flowers are aromatic. Season of interest: summer. Propagate by seed or softwood cuttings in spring. A physical barrier may be needed to keep cats away until plants are large enough to withstand their onslaughts. Winter treatment: prevent waterlogging.
RECOMMENDED VARIETIES: *Nepeta cataria* is the medicinal herb; *N.* 'Six Hills Giant' is a tall form; *N. sibirica* 'Souvenir d'André Chaudron' is lovely.

Nigella damascena **love-in-a-mist**
H: 60cm (2ft) S: 20cm (8in) ☀ ♦
Hardy annual for fertile, free-draining soil. Bright green foliage plant with blue, white or pink flowers and ornamental seed pods. Season of interest: summer. Propagate by seed in early autumn or spring. Scatter seed where it is to flower.
RECOMMENDED VARIETIES: *Nigella damascena* 'Miss Jekyll' has blue flowers; *N. damascena* 'Persian Jewels' is a mix of blue, white and pink.

Ocimum basilicum **basil**
H: 45cm (18in) S: 15cm (6in) ☀ ⊞ 🍴
Tender annual for moisture-retentive, free-draining soil. Green leaves with white flowers. Whole plant is aromatic. Season of interest: mid to late summer. Propagate from seed in early spring, with gentle heat and a dryish atmosphere, and plant out when all danger of frost has passed. Needs shelter from wind. Protect late-sown plants from cold in winter.
RECOMMENDED VARIETIES: *Ocimum basilicum* 'Green Ruffles' – green frilly leaves; *O. basilicum* 'Purple Ruffles' – purple frilly leaves; *O. basilicum* var. *purpurascens* – purple leaves.

Nigella damascena

Origanum **marjoram**
H: to 30cm (1ft) S: to 45cm (18in) ☀ 🦋 ⊞ 🍴
Variably hardy perennial for free-draining, alkaline soil. Flowers are pink, purple or white, depending on variety; leaves, which are aromatic, also vary in colour. Season of interest: summer. Propagate by softwood cuttings or division in spring. Gold-leaved forms need shade to prevent scorching. Those grown mainly for leaves can be trimmed regularly for a dense habit. Winter treatment: prevent waterlogging.
RECOMMENDED VARIETIES: *Origanum vulgare* 'Aureum' – yellow leaves, good groundcover; *O. laevigatum* 'Herrenhausen' – pink flowers; *Origanum* 'Rosenkuppel' has lovely dark flower buds.

Papaver **poppy, opium and field** H: to 75cm (2½ft) S: to 30cm (1ft) ☀ ☀ ⊞ 🍴 ☠
Hardy annual for moisture-retentive, free-draining soil. Grey or green foliage plant with flowers in a range of colours. Season of interest: summer. Propagate by seed in autumn or spring, in situ. Scatter seeds on soil surface – they need light to germinate.

Self-seeds readily, and may produce more than one generation per year. Thin or move (carefully) when small – they have fragile roots.
RECOMMENDED VARIETIES: *Papaver somniferum* – both single- and double-flowered forms are gorgeous; *P. rhoeas* (the field poppy) comes in various selected seed strains.
❋ The opium extracted from immature seedpods of *Papaver somniferum* is a dangerous drug, although ripe seeds are safe for culinary use.

Petroselinum crispum **parsley**
H: 40cm (16in) S: 20cm (8in) ☀ ☀ ⊞ 🍴 ☠
Hardy biennial for moisture-retentive, fertile soil. Bright green leaves with white flowers. Season of interest: all year. Propagate by seed from spring to late summer. Sow seed in modules if starting early, as it hates being disturbed. Protect from hot sun. Prone to occasional attack by slugs and snails. Winter treatment: protect from extreme cold and wet.
RECOMMENDED VARIETIES: two main types are grown, curled and flat, the latter having the best flavour. Moss-curled varieties are perhaps the most decorative.
❋ Avoid medicinal use when pregnant or if suffering from kidney disease.

Primula vulgaris **primrose**
H: 20cm (8in) S: 30cm (1ft) ☀ ☀ ⊞ 🍴 ☠
Hardy perennial for moisture-retentive, free-draining soil. Mid-green leaves with pale yellow, scented flowers. Season of interest: spring. Raise from seed sown in summer or divide clumps in late summer to early autumn. Primroses appreciate some shade in midsummer, and should be kept moist. Vine weevil larvae may eat roots – biological controls are available.
❋ Use only under qualified medical supervision. Can cause an allergic reaction; not to be taken if pregnant

Rosa gallica var. *officinalis*, *R. g.* 'Versicolor'
Apothecary's rose, rosa mundi,
H: to 80cm (2ft 9in) S: 1m (3ft 3in) ☼ ✚
Hardy deciduous shrub for fertile, moisture-retentive soil. Glossy green leaves with deep pink or pink-striped flowers. Season of interest: summer. Propagate from semi-ripe cuttings in summer or hardwood cuttings at leaf-fall. Nursery-raised plants have usually been grafted. Soil preparation is important – add plenty of well-rotted manure and rock phosphate. Prune new roses to about 15cm (6in) on planting.
RECOMMENDED VARIETIES: *Rosa gallica* var. *officinalis* is the true apothecary's rose (deep pink) and *R. gallica* 'Versicolor', the rosa mundi, is its sport, with striped flowers. Neither are repeat-flowering but both have a wonderful perfume.

Rosmarinus officinalis **rosemary** H: to 1.5m (5ft) S: to 1m (3ft 3in) ☼ ✖ ✚ ◆ |●|
Slightly tender evergreen shrub for free-draining soil. Dark green, aromatic leaves, some with yellow variegations, and flowers in shades of blue, pink or white. Season of interest: summer. Propagate from cuttings in spring or summer, or layer low-growing branches in summer. Prune lightly after flowering; remove frost-damaged branches. Winter treatment: protect from cold and wet.
RECOMMENDED VARIETIES: *Rosmarinus officinalis* 'Sissinghurst Blue' and *R. o.* 'Fota Blue' both have dark blue flowers; *R. o.* 'Miss Jessopp's Upright' is good for training as a standard; *R. o.* Prostratus Group and other prostrate forms are lovely but are less hardy than others.

Ruta graveolens **rue**
H: 60cm (2ft) S: 60cm (2ft) ☼ ✚ ☠
Hardy evergreen perennial for free-draining soil. Good blue-grey foliage plant with yellow flowers and aromatic

Papaver rhoeas

leaves. Season of interest: all year. Sow seed in spring; take cuttings in spring or summer. Prune in spring to maintain shape. Cutting off the flowers does no harm. Site away from paths.
RECOMMENDED VARIETIES: *Ruta graveolens* 'Jackman's Blue' is a good foliage form; *R. graveolens* 'Variegata', with cream markings, may be offered.
✱ Contact can cause skin to blister badly, especially in strong sun or when leaves are wet. Take only under medical supervision, as it can be highly toxic if used incorrectly. Do not take if pregnant.

Salvia officinalis **sage**
H: 60cm (2ft) S: 1m (3ft 3in) ☼ ✖ ✚ |●| ☠
Slightly tender evergreen perennial for free-draining, fertile soil. Green, purple or yellow-variegated foliage plant with blue flowers and aromatic leaves. Season of interest: early spring to late autumn. Raise from seed sown in spring, or from softwood cuttings or by layering in summer. Prune in summer (never in autumn) to encourage bushy growth.

Take cuttings in case of loss in a wet, cold winter. Prone to fungal diseases in damp conditions. Winter treatment: prevent waterlogging; protect young plants.
RECOMMENDED VARIETIES: *Salvia officinalis* 'Icterina' has yellow-splotched leaves; *S. o.* Purpurascens Group has purple leaves; *S. o.* 'Tricolor' has cream and pink variegations and is only half-hardy. *S. sclarea*, a taller hardy biennial, is easy to raise from seed.
✱ Sage can be toxic with prolonged medicinal use.

Santolina species and cultivars
cotton lavender
H: 40cm (16in) S: 60cm (2ft) ☼ ✚ ☠
Slightly tender evergreen shrub for free-draining soil. Excellent powdery grey or soft green foliage plant with yellow or cream flowers. Whole plant is aromatic. Season of interest: all year. Propagate by softwood cuttings or semi-ripe cuttings from early to late summer. Plants dislike wet conditions, and will survive much lower winter temperatures if kept dry. Prune hard in spring to maintain a bushy habit. Good for low hedges and tolerates frequent clipping. Winter treatment: protect from extremes of wet and cold.
RECOMMENDED VARIETIES: *Santolina chamaecyparissus* has lovely grey pipe-cleaner foliage but nasty bright yellow flowers; *S. serratifolia* has pretty cream flowers with grey-green foliage; *S. pinnata* ssp. *neapolitana* has green, finely divided foliage and pale yellow flowers.
✱ Do not take, except under qualified medical supervision.

Tanacetum parthenium **feverfew**
H: 60cm (2ft) S: 60cm (2ft) ☼ ✚ ☠
Hardy perennial for fertile soil. Good green or golden foliage plant with white and yellow daisy flowers. Whole plant is aromatic. Season of interest: spring to

autumn. Propagate by seed or division in spring, or take cuttings from early to mid-summer. Self-seeds prolifically, so dead-head if you want to avoid this.
RECOMMENDED VARIETIES: *Tanacetum parthenium* 'Aureum' is a golden-leaved form; *T. parthenium* 'White Bonnet' has pretty white double flowers.
✻ Can cause mouth ulcers and dermatitis. Use only under qualified medical supervision.

Tanacetum vulgare **tansy**
H: to 1m (3ft 3in) S: indefinite ☼ ☼ ✚ ♈ ☠
Hardy perennial for any soil type except boggy. Mid- to dark green foliage plant with yellow flowers and aromatic leaves. Season of interest: spring to autumn. Propagate by dividing plants in spring as new growth emerges, or by sowing seed in autumn under glass, or in spring outside. Invasive – grow in a buried pot to curb its spreading tendencies.
RECOMMENDED VARIETIES: *Tanacetum vulgare* var. *crispum* has curly foliage; the variegated forms – *T. v.* 'Isla Gold' and *T. v.* 'Silver Lace' – are less vigorous.
✻ A very powerful herb, which should only be taken under medical supervision and not at all during pregnancy.

Teucrium × *lucidrys* **wall germander**
H: 40cm (16in) S: 18cm (7in) ☼ ✚ ¦●¦ ☠
Hardy evergreen perennial for free-draining, alkaline soil. Dark green foliage with pink flowers. Leaves are aromatic when crushed. Season of interest: all year. Propagate by division or softwood cuttings in spring. Sometimes used for low hedging – plant 12–15cm (4–6in) apart and clip in spring and autumn.
RECOMMENDED VARIETIES: the variegated form is *T. chamaedrys* 'Variegatum' which is more tender than the plain green type.
✻ Use only under qualified medical supervision.

Rosmarinus officinalis

Thymus **thyme** H: varies, to 30cm (1ft) S: from 20cm (8in) to indefinite ☼ ✿ ✚ ¦●¦ ☠
Hardy to half-hardy evergreen perennial for free-draining, alkaline soil. Green, gold, variegated or silver foliage plant with mauve, pink or white flowers and aromatic leaves. Season of interest: summer. Propagate by cuttings taken throughout the summer. Thrives in poor soil, in a sunny, sheltered position. Creeping forms are nice among paving, but avoid areas of continuous foot traffic. Trim immediately after flowering to maintain compactness. Prevent waterlogging in winter.
RECOMMENDED VARIETIES: *Thymus* × *citriodorus* 'Silver Queen' has mauve-pink flowers and forms a low 15cm (6in) mound of white-edged foliage – although due to the smallness of the leaves the impression is of pale grey rather than distinct variegation. *T.* × *citriodorus* (lemon thyme) is another excellent culinary herb, the thyme flavour and perfume strongly overlaid with lemon. *T. vulgaris*, the common culinary thyme, forms a 15cm

(6in) mound, and has tiny dark green leaves and mauve flowers in summer.
✻ Avoid when pregnant. Use thyme oil only under medical supervision.

Tropaeolum majus **nasturtium**
H: 30cm–3m (1–10ft) S: to 1m (3ft 3in) ☼ ✚ ¦●¦ ☠
Hardy annual for free-draining soil. Good green or variegated foliage plant with yellow, orange or red flowers. Whole plant is aromatic. Season of interest: summer. Propagate by seed in spring, in situ. Thrives on poor soil, where it flowers more profusely than when well-fed. Prone to blackfly attack later in the season – spray with horticultural soap.
RECOMMENDED VARIETIES: *Tropaeolum majus* 'Alaska' is a low-growing variegated form; *T. majus* 'Hermine Grashof' is a tender perennial with double orange flowers, striking and rare – propagate from cuttings any time in growing season. Climbing varieties are sometimes offered.
✻ It is not a good idea to eat large quantities, no more than 30g (1oz) per day.

Verbascum thapsus **mullein**
H: to 2m (6½ft) S: to 1m (3ft 3in) ☼ ✚
Hardy biennial for free-draining soil. Silver-grey, woolly foliage plant with yellow flowers. Season of interest: mid to late summer. Raise from seed sown in spring or summer, or take root cuttings in winter. Winter treatment: prevent waterlogging.

Viola tricolor **heartsease, wild pansy**
H: 10cm (4in) S: 15cm (6in) ☼ ✚
Hardy short-lived perennial for free-draining soil. Mid-green leaves with purple and yellow flowers. Season of interest: spring to autumn. Propagate by seed in autumn or spring – do not cover seeds. Keep seedlings in a coldframe over winter. Self-seeds prolifically.

INDEX

AUTHOR'S ACKNOWLEDGMENTS

Many people helped and encouraged me during the writing of this book. I would particularly like to thank: Andrew Ford, Ann Freeman, Valerie Mitchell, Belinda and Martin Walker, Sarah Wyatt and all the gardeners and garden owners who so generously allowed us to photograph their herb gardens.

PUBLISHER'S ACKNOWLEDGMENTS

Conran Octopus would like to thank the following photographers and owners for their kind permission to reproduce the photographs in the book.

1 Sunniva Harte / Geffrye Museum, London; 2 Andrew Lawson / private garden, Oxfordshire (designer: Randall Anderson); 3 Vincent Motte; 4-5 S & O Mathews/Old Place Farm, Kent (original design: Anthony du gard Pasley); 6 Sunniva Harte / Hintelsham Hall, Suffolk; 8-9 Ursel Borstell / Philip van der Lee, Netherlands; 11 Marianne Majerus; 12 Deni Bown / The Herb Farm, Sonning Common, Berkshire; 13 John Glover / Hampton Court Flower Show (British Red Cross); 14 below Brigitte Perdereau; 14 above Gary Rogers; 15 below Patrick Mioulane / MAP; 15 above S & O Mathews / Brookwell, Surrey; 18 below Ursel Borstell; 18 above Marianne Majerus / Ballymaloe House, Co. Cork, Ireland; 19 Clive Boursnell / The Garden Picture Library / West Green House, Hampshire; 20 Jerry Harpur / Home Farm, Balscote, Oxfordshire; 21 Howard Rice /The Garden Picture Library; 22 above left Ursel Borstell/ Nursery Klaena Plantage, Aarnrom, Netherlands; 22 right Patrick Mioulane / MAP; 22 below left Vincent Motte; 25 Neil Campbell-Sharp; 26 below Dency Kane (designer: Dean Riddle); 26 above Sunniva Harte / Brook Cottage, Hampshire; 27 Marianne Majerus; 28 Neil Campbell- Sharp / 'Westwind' Marlborough, Hampshire; 29 above Claire de Virieu / Marie Claire Maison (stylist: Trebucq Mathilde); 30 Gary Rogers/Mr and Mrs Overstone's garden, The Cape, South Africa; 31 Linda Burgess / The Garden Picture Library; 32-33 Clive Boursnell / The Garden Picture Library / Barnsley House, Gloucestershire; 34 Tessa Traeger; 35 Didier Willery / The Garden Picture Library; 37 left Marianne Majerus / Holdenby House, Northamptonshire; 37 right Yann Monel / MAP; 39 S & O Mathews / North Court, Isle of Wight; 40 Marianne Majerus (designer: Mark Brown); 41 Michele Lamontagne; 42 Ursel Borstell; 43 Clive Boursnell / The Garden Picture Library; 44 Gary Rogers; 45 Juliette Wade/The Garden Picture Library / Alderley Grange, Gloucestershire; 46 below Jacqui Hurst / Kelly Castle, Fife, Scotland; 46 above S & O Mathews / R.H.S. Gardens, Wisley, Surrey; 47 Hugh Palmer / Country Homes and Interiors / Robert Harding Syndication; 48 Zara McCalmont / The Garden Picture Library; 49 Derek St. Romaine / Wyken Hall, Stanton, Suffolk (Sir Kenneth and Lady Carlisle); 50 Jerry Harpur / Iden Croft, Kent (designer: Simon Hopkinson); 51 Andrew Lawson / R.H.S. Chelsea Flower Show (Evening Standard Garden); 52 Andrew Lawson (Whichford Pottery); 53 left Helen Fickling (designer: Catherine Mason); 53 right Jacqui Hurst; 54 Helen Fickling (designer: Catherine Mason); 56 below Marianne Majerus / Judy's Country Garden, Lincolnshire; 56-57 Sunniva Harte / Hintelsham Hall, Suffolk; 58-61 Marianne Majerus / Judy's Country Garden, Lincolnshire; 62 Sunniva Harte / Hintelsham Hall, Suffolk; 64-66 Sunniva Harte / Old Place Farm, Kent (original design by: Anthony du gard Pasley); 68 Stephen Robson / Fanner Green, Essex; 70-72 Sunniva Harte / The Geffrye Museum, London; 74-76 Marianne Majerus / Ballymaloe Cookery School, Co. Cork, Ireland; 78-80 Sunniva Harte / Brook Cottage, Hampshire; 82-84 Andrew Lawson (designer: Randall Anderson); 87 right Deni Bown; 87 left Christian Sarramon; 88 Andrew Lawson; 89 Deni Bown; 90 John Glover; 91 S & O Mathews; 92 Derek St. Romaine; 93 Michele Lamontagne